LIFE INSURANCE UNDERWRITING
A Practical Insight

LIFE INSURANCE UNDERWRITING
A Practical Insight

DR. KANINIKA MISHRA
Life Underwriter Training Council Fellow,
Associate Financial Planner

DEEP & DEEP PUBLICATIONS PVT. LTD.
F-159, Rajouri Garden, New Delhi - 110 027

LIFE. INSURANCE UNDERWRITING
A Practical Insight

ISBN 978-81-8450-185-8

Printed in India at MAYUR ENTERPRISES
WZ Plot No. 3, Gujjar Market, Tihar Village, New Delhi - 110 018

Published by DEEP & DEEP PUBLICATIONS PVT. LTD.,
F-159, Rajouri Garden, New Delhi - 110 027 • Phone: 25435369, 25440916
E-mail: ddpubs@gmail.com • ddpbooks@yahoo.co.in
Showroom:
2/13, Ansari Road, Daryaganj, New Delhi - 110 002 • Telefax: 23245122

Contents

Part II
NON-MEDICAL, FINANCIAL AND MEDICAL UNDERWRITING

PART V
SAMPLE UNDERWRITING SOLUTIONS

Atal Bihari Vajpayee

MESSAGE

I am glad to know that Dr. Kaninika Mishra has written a book titled **Life Insurance Underwriting—A Practical Insight.**

I hope the book would be useful for all who are connected with life insurance.

I extend my best wishes to the writer and also for the successful publication of the book.

(A.B. Vajpayee)

New Delhi
November 12, 2008

6A, Krishna Menon Marg, New Delhi 110011 India
Tel.: +91 11 23015308, 23793877 Fax: +91 11 23794612

Preface

Life insurance, being a cooperative device to spread the loss caused by an uncertain event in the interest of the insured, is and will always remain an important part of financial services business. The recent economic liberalization policies of the Government of India have resulted in bringing this, heretofore, low key industry into the limelight. This has also set the stage for advent of many multinational companies with new strategies in areas of life insurance marketing, distribution and product-mix. Due to sharp media focus, increased awareness and phenomenal growth rates life insurance has become an important discipline of study in the field of business management. Albeit quite a bit of literature is now available on life insurance *per se*, however the aspects of life insurance underwriting are still scantly written about. There is, therefore, a pressing need, for the benefit of current and future readers, to analyze and write about this hub of life insurance operations and practice. This book is an attempt to fulfil this need in an easy and logical way to serve the requirement of students and professionals by providing them a useful insight in all practical aspects of underwriting the risks in life insurance.

Many educational institutes are now teaching insurance either as a main course or as a part of an overall management program. Most of these courses have underwriting as one of the subjects. Students who complete courses in Insurance discipline find employment in insurance companies where they have to deal directly or indirectly with the underwriting process. With its focus on the applied aspects of underwriting function, the text is designed to prepare students to take up a career in Life Insurance industry.

It is also intended here to guide sales persons, risk managers and other professionals in the industry and enable them to become aware of the concepts, philosophy and methods of underwriting. It gives an insight into the key aspects of the client's medical and financial profile that influence decision on premium and acceptance of the client's application for insurance.

The subject of underwriting is discussed here in a progressive step by step manner starting with the concept of risk in insurance and the fundamentals of insurance premium and risk classification. The introductory chapter of the book deals with the theory of life insurance and its general principles and practices. This forms a basis for discussion of advanced concepts of life insurance in the later parts of the book. However, the book assumes some basic knowledge about life insurance principles and will well serve a readership seeking to explore the specialized area of life insurance underwriting.

Underwriting of a life insurance policy can be appropriately divided into three parts. These are non-medical, financial and medical underwriting. While there are significant interplays and fusions between these parts, the book addresses each one distinctly and in a sequential manner for easy comprehension of the readers. Part I deals with basic principles and concepts of underwriting. Part II discusses non-medical underwriting, financial underwriting and medical underwriting. Part III contains details of new developments in this field.

Life insurance policies do at times become contentious. The beneficiaries take recourse to legal actions for redressal of their grievances. Many a times, the core principles of insurance and underwriting policies are at the center of the legal arguments. This thus obligates the insurers as well as the insured to comprehend the correct tenets of law while entering into the contract for life insurance. Part IV covers this legal aspect. It contains the synopsis of three actual Supreme Court and Delhi High Court cases on various causes of actions related to life insurance policies. These revealing cases would help in grasping the do's and don'ts by the contracting parties where the life insurance underwriters happen to be essential performers.

Part V, the last part, includes seven sample underwriting solutions for the guidance of the life insurance underwriting professionals.

The annexure attached at the end of the book contains some useful sample guidelines and important information of use in life insurance underwriting.

It is hoped that the readers will find the book professionally valuable and practically useful.

DR. KANINIKA MISHRA

PART I

CONCEPTS, PRINCIPLES AND PROCESSES

Chapter 1

Introduction to Life Insurance Underwriting

Learning Objectives

The material in this chapter should enable the reader to understand

- ❖ Basic Concepts, Definitions and Principles of Underwriting
- ❖ Life Insurance Pricing and Premium Components
- ❖ Types of Risks Relevant for Underwriting Assessment
- ❖ Three Categories of Underwriting Decisions—Standard, Sub-standard and Rejected

CHAPTER

1

Introduction to Life Insurance Underwriting

BASIC CONCEPTS AND DEFINITIONS

Underwriting in a broad sense refers to the process that a large financial service provider, either a bank or an insurance company uses to provide access to products such as credit (loan) or insurance to a customer. Historically, the term originated from marine insurance and was used in its literal meaning where the person who assumed liability for damage to the ship or its cargo during transit would sign his name at the foot of the agreement. This trend of 'writing under' the agreement, to share or assume the risk, liability or loss led to the term "underwriter". With the passage of time the individuals were replaced by companies who were ready to take on a part of the risk (risk in this context means the probability of loss), however, the term underwriter continued to mean the same—'someone who selected or rejected risks'.

In the banking sector, underwriting is concerned with detailed credit analysis preceding the granting of a loan, based on information furnished by the borrower, such as employment history, salary and financial statements. In life insurance companies, the underwriting process is one of the most important processes as unlike the banking industry where the bank is compensated in case of non-payment of the loan through guarantors or collaterals, such protection does not exist for the life insurance business.

Life insurance provides a sum of money called 'death benefit' upon the death of the insured person in return for small periodic payments called premiums. Insurance is a financial arrangement that redistributes the costs of unexpected losses. Insurance involves the transfer of potential losses to an insurance pool (group of insured people). The pool combines all the potential losses and then transfers the cost of the predicted losses back to those exposed. Thus, insurance involves the transfer of loss exposures to an insurance pool and the redistribution of losses among members of the pool.[1]

The insurance companies compute premium on the probability of death in the population. If there are more deaths than those estimated the company incurs losses and in extreme situations can even become bankrupt. Thus underwriting or selecting only those individuals for insurance who are expected to have an average life span becomes very critical for life insurance companies. Hence it is of importance to note that life expectancy by all measures is exclusively individual and it is not possible to create a premium table for each life insurance seeker and consequently insurance companies design a premium table based on the life span of an average individual in a population for different life insurance products/plans.

The sale of a life insurance policy is not complete till the application is 'underwritten'. No proposal for insurance can be accepted without an analysis by the underwriters who decide whether to accept the risk or not. In spite of the critical role it plays in the life insurance risk management there is a general lack of awareness about underwriting principles and procedures. The sales persons selling life insurance policies, doctors examining the applicants and even the clients purchasing life insurance products, need to be fully aware of the underwriting parameters in life insurance, so that the insurance process is completed smoothly.

Risk Selection and Classification

Underwriting is defined as the method of evaluation and assessment of each life insurance application and then making a determination of whether the applicant can be insured and if yes, at what premium rates. The underwriters are the assessors of risk and take decisions on each and every case (application) that comes to their desk.

The underwriting consists of two processes, selection process and classification process. The selection process involves evaluation and assessment of each life insurance application and then making a determination of whether the applicant can be insured or not. The underwriter takes this decision based on the financial and medical characteristics of the applicant as also the underwriting policy of the company and its risk-taking capacity.

Individual applicants who are deemed as acceptable risks represent unique varying profiles, backgrounds and health conditions. Therefore, a classification process is used to determine the degree of risk of every applicant and each applicant is assigned a particular risk category known as 'risk class'. By classification underwriters make sure that insured individuals with homogenous loss potential (i.e. similar probability of death) are placed in a distinct class paying a premium corresponding to the degree of risk they represent. Each class of insured individuals bears a fair share of losses and expenses in proportion to the overall group of insured people (insurance pool) in the company.

The classification process of underwriting has mathematical implications. If an underwriter places an insured representing a certain risk level in a higher risk class than appropriate then the insured ends up paying more than his share of fair price. This means that the insured is actually subsidizing the cost of insurance for others in the risk pool which makes insurance unfair and unequal for people in the insurance pool. Albeit it must be noted that some degree of subsidization will occur since the risk classes themselves represent a large number of insureds who are unique individuals who would also have some differences even though the risk class is defined based on many of their similar characteristics. The different risk classes and their classification are discussed in detail in chapter 6 on medical underwriting.

Principle of Insurable Interest

For insurance to operate effectively the insured should have an incentive to prevent or at least regret the loss. If the insured is indifferent to loss then the insurance pool will experience more loss than predicted. The increased losses in turn will require higher insurance premiums and soon many insured will not be able to afford insurance and the system will collapse. For this reason insurance law requires insureds to demonstrate that the insured event represents a loss to them. In case of non-life or general insurance when insuring a property, it is vital for the insurance company to establish that the individual who has taken the insurance policy for a property has an insurable interest in the property. The policy is, therefore, issued only if the applicant is the owner of the property and stands to suffer a direct financial loss if there is damage to the property.

In life insurance, an applicant is the owner of the policy when he* applies for insurance on his own life or when he applies for or proposes insurance on another person. If he takes a policy on his own life, as per insurance law a nominee has to be named who is entitled to receive the death benefit on death of the insured. People are assumed to have unlimited insurable interest in their own lives and in such cases the underwriter checks the relationship with the nominee to determine insurable interest.

In case an applicant proposes life insurance on another person, he is entitled to receive death benefits on death of the insured person. In such cases insurable interest between the insured and the policy owner is a must to have a valid contract. The law recognizes the following relationships as having insurable interest:

- Husband and wife have unlimited insurable interest in each others life.
- Parents on life of their children.

---

* The applicant has been referred to as 'he' or 'his' in most instances in this book for sake of simplicity. It means any person related to the context male or female.

- A creditor has insurable interest in the life of a debtor to the extent of the amount involved plus a reasonable amount of interest.
- Partners in a business have insurable interest in the lives of their co-partners.
- A company has insurable interest in the lives of the key employees of the company.

Though it is said that a person has unlimited interest in his own life or life of his spouse, it may be noted that insurable interest must be a pecuniary (economic) interest and it is measured by the extent of financial loss which the family of the insured will suffer in the event of his death. Thus insurable interest, in cases where the insurance is on self or spouse, is limited to the extent of monetary loss of income to the family on death of the insured. In cases where a company proposes insurance on the life of a key employee or partner the underwriter has to make sure that the death benefit amount does not exceed the estimated loss of profits to the company in the event of the insured's death. Financial underwriting is the method followed to evaluate the suitable amount of insurance that can be offered to individuals or business applicants.[2] Therefore a very important and key concept that the underwriter has to evaluate while underwriting is the 'insurable interest'. This is further discussed in detail in chapter 4.

COMPONENTS OF LIFE INSURANCE PREMIUM

The insurance company has a table of premium rates for the average insured population for each product line.[3] The premium is a function of the average life span of individuals in a population. Insurance companies use mortality tables[4] to estimate as to how long an average person of a given age is expected to live. These tables are based trends in large numbers of people and cannot, of course, predict how long any one particular individual will live. The mortality table lists the probability of death for persons of all ages before they reach their next birthday. This probability given.as (qx) in the table is calculated by a mathematical formula which uses number of people alive at the beginning of the age interval and the number dying during the age interval. The mortality table represents the death rate for a person of a specific age with average health.

It is not possible to have different mortality tables for different people with different conditions of health, habits, regions, etc. Therefore, a standard mortality table in respect of people having a particular set of factors affecting health is drawn. For those who do not conform to this standard due to bad health or other reasons, premium is adjusted based on the mortality they are likely to experience. Such people are assigned a different risk class during underwriting. The premium rate for the average insured person is based on a prediction of losses or deaths in the insurance pool. *The responsibility to reduce any differences between this prediction and the actual claims experience of the company rests with the underwriter.*

Insurance companies rely on actuarial mathematics to compile data based on the mortality tables and develop insurance premium rates for different products. Actuaries review past statistics and project future results. Using the data from mortality tables the actuaries predict the number of people insured by the company will die in a given year. They also predict the expenses of the company and interest earnings of premiums received by policy owners to develop a final premium table for each product. The following are the four building blocks that constitute insurance premiums:

- Actual cost of losses (claims to be paid out based on mortality rate in the population).
- Expenses of operating and maintaining insurance pool.
- Allowance for unexpected loss.
- Earnings on investment of collected premiums.

Good risk selection and classification lies in ensuring that only those applicants who have an average risk of death are given insurance at the normal premium rates as per the premium table and those with higher risks are charged higher premiums based on their risk classification.

Another important factor to obtain a predictive accuracy of loss in an insurance pool is the need of a substantial number of individual units This is called *'the law of large numbers'*. It states that the insurer's or insurance company's loss prediction becomes more accurate as the number of insureds in the risk pool increases. Each group or class of risk also has to have a sufficient number of people in the class to have an accurate loss outcome similar to the probability of loss.

TYPES OF RISKS RELEVANT FOR UNDERWRITING

The word risk has been used many times in this chapter so far and its meaning from the underwriting perspective denotes the degree or probability of loss. So a person who is suffering from cancer is supposed to be a greater risk as he has more probability of death than a healthy person.

Fundamentally, risks are categorized based on the possible outcomes of an event. Risks can be divided into pure risks and speculative risks. *Pure risks* are those which cannot result in any gain. *Speculative risks* are those where there may be gain or loss due to the event. Risks of death, injury or damage to property are pure risks as these events invariably cause loss to the sufferer and cannot attribute any gain. Risks taken in investing in stock market or risks taken in gambling are speculative risks as they may result in either a gain or a loss in the transaction. Insurance can be taken only on pure risks. Speculative risks are not insurable (uninsurable). An insurance policy taken with an intention of gaining out of it is called a wagering (gambling) contract and is invalid as it goes against the concept of insurable interest. As explained earlier in this chapter to ensure that insurable interest exists underwriters make certain that beneficiaries of the policy have a monetary interest in the life of the insured and the amount of insurance does not exceed the extent of loss. Lack of insurable interest in an insurance contract makes the policy invalid even if such a policy is inadvertently issued by a life insurance company.

The underwriter uses a host of information to select and classify the applicants for life insurance policies. Most of this information comes from the applicant himself. Thus, risk assessment cannot be accurate if the applicant lies, conceals or withholds information. Hiding or distorting information affecting risk appraisal may lead to an increase in the probability of loss experienced in the insurance pool. Any act of an applicant aimed at hiding financial information, overstating income or understating age or being dishonest about health or other variables which affect risk assessment is called *moral hazard*.[5]

Types of Risks that Increase Possibility of Death

The three basic risks that the underwriters look for, which increase the possibility of death, are : (i) disease, (ii) accident, and (iii) risk of lapse of the policy or fraud due to financial problems of the client.

Box 1.1

The basic Principle behind the Underwriting Process is 'Higher the Risk-higher the Premium'

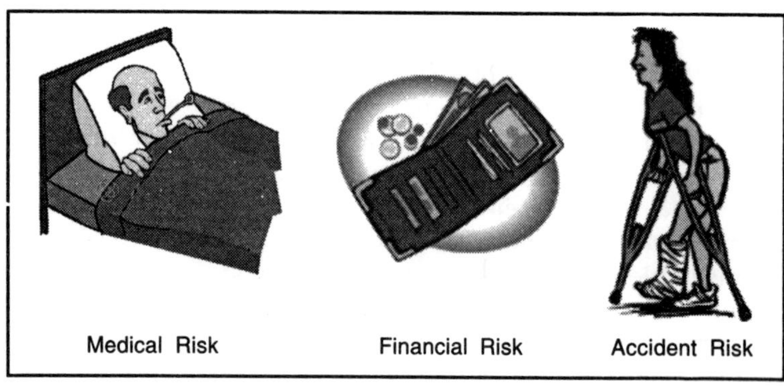

Medical Risk Financial Risk Accident Risk

Risk of Diseases

As seen in the mortality table in annexure 2, mortality increases with the increase in age. This is due to vulnerability to various diseases associated with increase in age. This risk is offset by the increasing normal premium rates according to age as seen from the premium table chart in annexure 1. The risk classification process requires the underwriters to determine any deviation from normal health in the applicants and also place them in different risk categories.

The underwriter searches for information in the application form that impacts the life span of a person and increases the likelihood of death. Diseases such as heart disease,

Box 1.2

Age is the Fundamental Factor that Affects Risk of Disease

cancers, etc. are known to decrease life spans and, therefore, any indication in the application form of such diseases is investigated thoroughly by the underwriter. The underwriter also looks for potential factors (information) that might result in the client having a disease at a later stage in case the client does not have any disease presently. For example, if a woman applies for insurance and mentions in the application form that her sister and mother both have had breast cancer, the underwriter may charge an extra premium as medical research proves that the risk of breast cancer increases if a person's family members (mother/sisters) have suffered from it.

Box 1.3

Risk from Diseases

Existing Disease	*Possibility of Future Disease*
Diagnosed already/on treatment	Symptoms Present not diagnosed
	Family members having a disease
	Smoking or heavy drinking habit

The underwriter ignores the history of diseases which do not affect life span such as common cold, minor skin diseases, etc. If the client is suffering from a very serious disease or critical ailments and death is almost certain the underwriter rejects the application and the company does not issue any life insurance policy. Conditions such as advanced stage cancer, HIV (Human Immunodeficiency Virus) positive are usually declined life insurance. In some instances complicated cases of heart disease or diabetes also result in rejection of an application for life insurance.

Risk from Accident

The other risk that the underwriter looks for is the presence of an increased probability of risk of accidents. Though any individual can have an accident irrespective of social status, health, or age, but certain services, occupations or hobbies increase the chances of risk. Bomb disposal experts, circus trick performers and mine workers are examples of people with increased risk of accidents which enhance the probability of death due to their jobs. People with adventure sport hobbies such as sky diving, gliding, scuba diving, etc. are also carefully evaluated by underwriters to assess their potential risk of accidental deaths. The region or country of residence can also increase the risk of death in accidents due to civil riots and terrorism. In some cases country of residence may pose health risks to the resident, e.g., from land mines laid by the fighting factions in a civil war.

Box 1.4

- Accident risks generally do not increase with increase in age
- Accident risks increase due to risky occupations, hobbies or residential location

Risk due to Financial Reasons

Another factor that can give rise to potential losses to the company is the client's financial inability to pay the premium which may lead to discontinuation or lapse of the policy. High number of policy lapses affects the insurance company financially, as there is a high acquisition cost associated with the sale of an insurance policy. Aspects of insurable interest and moral hazard have to be kept in mind while underwriting to ensure that the insurance amount is commensurate with the applicant's actual financial worth.

Forgery is common in financial documentation. Applicants may attempt to get higher amounts of life insurance issued with intention to defraud. Some cases of suicide by life insurance policy-holders have been documented. In situations of acute financial distress the policy-holder may commit suicide so that the life insurance benefit can be used by their families (nominees) to get out of the financial crisis. There have also been cases where clients have fabricated stories of their own death to claim life insurance death benefits. The financial well being of the client is assessed to ensure that he/she has enough funds and resources to pay the premiums and to guard against fraudulent claims due to deaths as a result of financial problems.

Box 1.5
Financial Risks

❖ Lapse of Policy	❖ Fraud

UNDERWRITING DECISION-RISK CATEGORIES

The previous section has enumerated the types of risks that the underwriter looks at for an underwriting decision. Based on evaluation of these risks, the underwriter's aim is to protect the company against loss and early claims by placing insureds in appropriate risk class/category and charging extra premiums for higher risk classes/categories.

If a particular applicant's risk of death is so high that the probability of death in effect becomes a certainty, the person is no longer insurable (uninsurable). Underwriters also decline or reject applications of those who are uninsurable on account of lack of insurable interest.

Underwriters divide life insurance applications into three broad categories of risk, i.e. Standard Risks, Substandard Risks and Rejected Risks.

Standard Risks

When the underwriter after careful examination of potential risks finds that the client does not have any additional risk (i.e. the risk or chance of death is the same as expected for an average individual of that age as per the mortality table) then the policy is issued at regular premium rates (*standard rates*). This premium is the same as given in premium tables of the insurance company.

Substandard Risks

In early days of life insurance it was sufficient for a person to appear before the board of directors who assessed his health by appearance and issued the policy if they found that he looked healthy. With the progress of medical science and the advanced techniques of investigations into the impact of different variables of health on mortality it was found that the inherent problems in health significantly affected the number of claims paid out by the company and thus the profitability of the company. Thus a system of medical examination evolved and the process of medical tests for life insurance policies began. From the result of medical tests and examinations for each applicant it was found that the health status of applicants ranged from slight unhealthy to serious unhealthy conditions. Subsequently different classes of "substandard risk" classification and a system to determine extra premium for each substandard group was devised. Accordingly if the underwriter finds an additional risk, and a higher probability of death than for an average individual of the same age, the percentage of extra risk or 'extra mortality' is calculated for the particular risk which the client is exposed to.[6]

The underwriting manuals, form the back-bone of the system used to calculate the extra premium. It lists almost all possible causes of death by diseases or accidents and also gives the *Extra Mortality Rate* (EMR) for each condition. The mortality data available from life insurance, epidemiological studies and clinical literature over the years have been used to determine the effect of various factors that determine life span. Underwriting manuals have been compiled based on these data.

The manuals are continuously upgraded to reflect the changes in disease patterns and mortality predictions.

Risk Calculation Principles

The basic principle for risk calculation is to assign a numerical value to each factor that determines longevity. Average mortality as per mortality table for each age group is taken as 100. Debit points are given for unfavorable factors like tobacco use, pre-existing health conditions and weight problems, etc. Credit points are given for favorable features like proportionate body weight, normal blood pressure and healthy family history. The net rating is calculated. The excess of this rating over 100 is taken as Extra Mortality Rating (EMR). For example, if a 35 year old person with a height of 165 cm and weight of 100 kgs applies for life insurance policy, the underwriter can clearly define him as overweight which is one of the risk factors for many diseases. If the underwriter finds that his family medical history, stated in the application form is better than 'average' and he does not smoke or drink and on medical examination is found to have high blood pressure his rating as per company's underwriting manual may be computed as per the following:

Illustration:

Base Mortality Value 100

Factor	Extra Mortality Debit/Credit
Blood pressure	+50
Overweight	+25
No smoking	–15
Good family history	–10
Total +50 Extra Mortality Rate (EMR) above base value of	100)[7]

Based on the above system of rating insurance companies classify individual applicants in different risk classes with EMRs in sets of twenty-five. Therefore, the different substandard risk classes into which the underwriter classifies risks are +25, +50, +75, +100, etc. The insurance companies charge additional premium for each particular EMR, which is called loading or rating, based on a specific formulae. This formula is a combination of applicant's age and the product he has applied for. The higher premium rate (*substandard premium rate*) is charged in order to provide for the possibility of shorter than average life span of the client.

Chapter 6 of this book 'Medical Underwriting' gives an overview of common diseases and the percentage of extra premium to be charged by the underwriter for each disease. This chapter also gives the detailed explanation on the premium components and how extra mortality causes the increase in the premiums for clients of different age groups and different types of insurance plans.

Rejected Cases—Declined Cases

If the health of the client is very poor and the probability of death is very high (EMR above 400 or 500) life insurance companies do not offer insurance to the applicant and the case is *declined* (rejected). Diseases such as cancer, Human Immunodeficiency Virus (HIV) infection, kidney failure, etc. fall in this category. The list of such diseases which are commonly not accepted for insuring applicants by life insurance companies are given under 'Medical Underwriting' in Chapter 6.

Rejected Cases—Postponed Cases

Some times the underwriter decides to *postpone* a case. This means that the client cannot be insured at that point of time. However, he can be insured at a later date based on fresh medical tests. The common reasons for postponed cases are discussed in chapter 6 : 'Medical Underwriting'.

Preferred Rates

Some companies have a *Preferred rate* where an exceptionally healthy person can get a lower than normal premium. In general, preferred rates are offered to applicants in excellent health, with very few or no risk factors.

Box 1.6

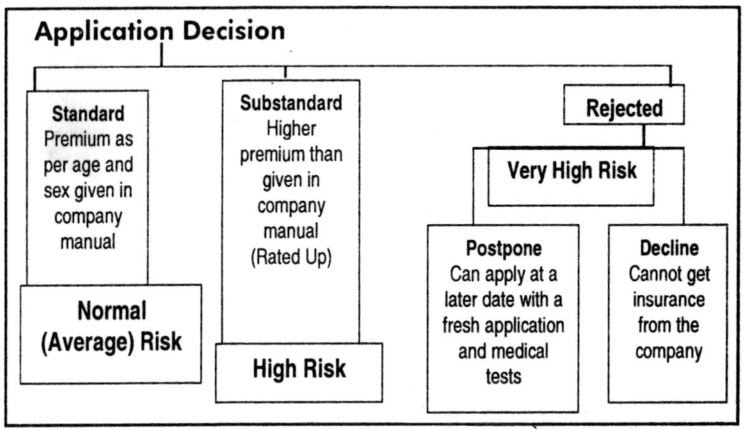

People in the standard risk range are regarded as having mortality expectations which are average and hence they get entitled to insurance at standard rates. Most of the applications for life insurance are issued at standard premium rates, only a small number of applications are given substandard rates and even fewer are declined or postponed. The companies generally try to maintain the ratio of 90:7:3 between standard, substandard and rejected cases because excessive number of rejections or substandard policies affect the morale of the sales force. It also increases cost of doing business and causes loss of good will among the insurable public.

Box 1.7

Decisions Percentage in Insurance Companies[8]

Standard	90%	Substandard	7%	Rejection (Decline/Postpone)	3%

Notes and References

1. Introduction to Risk Management and Insurance, Eighth Edition by Mark S. Dorfman, 2005 Prentice-Hall Inc.
2. Reference-CFP2, Risk Management and Insurance Planning, International College of Financial Planning Limited, 2002.
3. Premium table for some products of Life Insurance Corporation of India (LIC) is given in Annexure 1.

4. LIC Mortality table which is used by all companies in India as a base to calculate premium rates is given in Annexure 2.
5. Introduction to Risk Management and Insurance, Eighth Edition by Mark S. Dorfman, 2005, Prentice-Hall Inc.
6. Insurance Underwriting: A Managerial Perspective, Vol. III, 2002, ICFAI University Press.
7. This is only an Illustration, for indicative EMRs of specific medical conditions. Please refer to Chapter No. 6 on Medical Underwriting.
8. *Source*: USA AED Foundation; Term Life America Underwriting; The Department of Health and Human Services, USA.

Chapter 2

The Process of Underwriting Decision-making

Learning Objectives

The material in this chapter should enable the reader to understand

- Underwriting Guidelines
- Factors that influence underwriting decisions
- Sources of information for the underwriters
- Underwriting process flow

CHAPTER

2

The Process of Underwriting Decision-making

INFORMATION REQUIRED FOR RISK SELECTION

The availability of information about the life insurance applicant is vital for the underwriting function. A sound underwriting decision can be taken only when sufficient information is available about risk factors that impact life span of the applicant. The underwriter needs to focus only on significant risks during the risk selection process. Significant risks are those risks which are not common to all those seeking life insurance. Common risks are taken into account to determine the expected loss to the whole insurance pool. Such risks are reflected in the life insurance company's mortality tables and hence built into the premiums. For example, the life span of an average individual in India is lesser than the life span of an average individual in the developed countries and therefore such risks are reflected in Indian mortality rates. However, having a family history of diabetes, smoking or being overweight increase the risk of early death and, therefore, these factors become significant for the underwriters. The degree of risk factors is also important. Minor risks generally can be overlooked but larger risks which adversely impact the life span cannot be ignored. Consequently a slight extra weight would be a minor risk, while being overweight along with smoking and a risky family history are significantly larger risk for the underwriter to ignore. Some of these risk factors can be discerned from medical tests while some may be ascertained from information available in the client's application form. These guiding considerations and other important risk factors that the underwriters need to assess are discussed in succeeding paragraphs.

Underwriting Information Guidelines

Information which indicates the risk factors is critical for the underwriting process. However, due to constraints of time, resources and the privacy regulations underwriters get only limited information about the risk indicators. Therefore, an underwriter has to decide as to how much information is to be gathered and on what specific aspects. To a large extent these aspects are pre-defined by the life insurance companies. The companies do specify the kinds of information the underwriters must collect for assessing the case for each life insurance applicant. Such guidelines are directly linked to the applicant's age, income, insurance and the product applied for. These underwriting guidelines spell out the documents required with each individual application.

Insurance companies construct basic underwriting guidelines as per the following structure.

- *Age of Applicant*: Higher the age, higher the risk of diseases therefore detailed and specific medical information is required for older applicants.
- *Type of product and Sum assured*[1]: More risky the product, more information is sought from the applicant. Higher the amount of death benefit means more risk for the company and therefore more investigations will be needed into the financial aspects and medical conditions of the applicant.

- *Type of client to be insured*: Women and children are prone to specific diseases and therefore a different set of medical tests may be required for them.
- *Regulations*: Micro-insurance or policies for rural market may be very small to justify medical tests or extensive information. Therefore, they would need simple underwriting guidelines.

The underwriting guidelines serve two main purposes. Firstly, they provide consistency in information received for underwriting and secondly ensure uniformity in underwriting decisions. For example, the underwriting guideline may stipulate that all applicants between the ages of 36 to 40 years applying for life insurance of Rs. 20 lacs or above need to undergo certain medical tests and also submit their income tax returns. This will ensure that applicants in similar age group and sum assured have matching supporting information. This leads to consistency in decision-making across the life insurance company amongst different underwriters. It may be noted that the underwriters can and do call for additional information apart from those mentioned in underwriting guidelines if they either find the available information inadequate or need a more definite information about any anticipated life risk for the applicant. However, the rule which the underwriters follow is that the additional information to be called for should be convenient to obtain and also cost effective to acquire.

The core underwriting parameters of insurance companies comprise of the medical and the financial guidelines. The medical guidelines specify the age and insurance amount criteria for determining whether a medical test is required and if yes which tests have to be undergone by the applicant. The financial guidelines, stipulate as to what financial documents are required based on the sum assured.

As a rule the medical information requirements increase with the increase in age and similarly financial information requirements increase with the increase in the sum assured. When the sum assured is low, it would not be cost effective to send the applicant for expensive medical tests. Consequently, the application comes under the non-medical category and the underwriter has to base his assessment of the client's risk on the information given in the application form as also the agent's[2] report, etc.

Apart from the medical and financial guidelines, underwriting guidelines specify information requirements for specific risk profiles such as those engaged in certain risk prone occupations. For ascertaining such risk profiles certain questionnaires or documents are required which help underwriters to identify the specific factors that attract cognizable risk in life insurance cases. For example, in case of a pilot, aviation questionnaire may be a mandatory underwriting requirement which elicits details like the type of plane flown by the applicant, number of hours spent in flying, etc. Depending on these facts, underwriters can concentrate on the relevant areas and uniformly take decisions for all pilots.

Factors that Impact Risk

Extra body weight, smoking, drinking and state of health are certain factors which impact mortality in human beings. The underwriting guidelines facilitate the search and collection of such information to assess applicant's risk factors and put him into the appropriate category of extra premium. While doing so information must be gathered on every factor that might adversely affect his life span. Combined effect of all risk factors is also assessed as there is interrelationship between various factors that may impact overall risk component.

To evaluate the factors that increase mortality risk, the basic information available to the underwriter is found in the application form, in the questionnaires and in other details tendered by the agent or the applicant. The life insurance application form also contains medical questions and declarations about applicant's general health. The underwriter also has access to medical reports, medical questionnaires and doctor's examination results in the cases requiring medical examination. The non-medical factors like age, occupation, financial status, etc. also impact the life expectancy. Such information is available to the underwriters from the application form, as also the prior insurance applications if any and other non-medical documents submitted by the applicants.

Box 2.1
Factors that Increase Risk of Death (Mortality)

Medical Factors	*Non-medical Factors*
Over-weight	Advancing Age
Tobacco smoking or chewing	Risky Occupation
Excessive Alcohol Drinking	Hazardous Hobbies
Adverse Family History	Risky Residential Environment
Adverse Medical History	Abject Financial Status

SOURCES OF UNDERWRITING INFORMATION

The factors of risk assessment outlined in the foregoing discussion need to be elicited in order to arrive at the underwriting decision. Applicant himself, along with the agent/ sales person, the doctor in cases where a medical test has been done, or a verification agency if engaged are the various sources that can be used for this purpose. Each of these information source is discussed in detail in subsequent paragraphs.

Box 2.2
Underwriting Information Sources and Tools

Sources		*Tools*
Client/Applicant	→	Application Form and Financial Documents
Agent	→	Agent's Report
Doctor	→	Medical Report/Medical Test Reports
Verification Agency	→	Verification Report

The Applicant

The information supplied by the client in the application form is an important and statutory source of information for assessment of risk by the underwriter. The application carries an undertaking from the applicant that all the facts stated by him are true and correct. It thus becomes a part of the legal insurance contract document after the policy is issued. Different life insurance companies have different formats of insurance applications but the content and the questions are generally the same.

Most application forms consist of two main sections. *First section* contains details about the non-medical factors and the *second section* has questions related to the medical history of the client. The non-medical part of the application covers personal details such as name, identity proof, address and place and date of birth. These details establish the identity and the age of the client which is an important requirement for the issue of an insurance policy.[3]

Other non-medical questions in the first part of the application relate to the occupation, hobbies and the domicile, viz. whether the client is living in a foreign country. Names of nominees and details of the sum assured and the premium amount being paid are also asked for in this part of the application form. The application has questions about the client's insurance history including details of all life insurance policies already in force, and whether any earlier applications were declined or issued at substandard rates.

The second section consists of the family history of the client with details and ages of all family members.[4] The client has to mention the intensity of smoking or drinking if applicable and also if he or she has had any surgery or major medical interventions in the past. This section also consists of a list of questions regarding various diseases which have to be answered in affirmative or negative. This part of the application also asks several other related groups of questions. Details of the applicant's health record including illnesses, injuries and surgical operations, usually within last 10 years are asked for. In respect of female applicants an additional question about pregnancy is mandated.

As per life insurance regulations all questions have to be completed in the client's own handwriting and signed. The agent cannot and should not fill in the application forms. The applicant's signature is generally witnessed by the agent.[5]

Box 2.3
Information Generally asked for in the Life Insurance Application Form

Non-medical Information	*Medical Information*
• Identification Details	• Personal Medical history
• Age	• Specific body/organ functions
• Occupation and recent work history	• Family health history
• Income	• Physicians consulted within last 5 years
• Amount and type of life insurance policy applied for	• Use of alcohol
• Intended nominee	• Smoking habit
• Existing insurance, if any	

The Agent

An agent is a key source of information for an underwriter. He* is an important player in faster and effective underwriting decision-making. If the agent's report is exhaustive, accurate, all inclusive and precise the underwriting decisions will be fast, fair and faultless. Some companies require the agent to file a declaration on certain informative details. These are generally, as to how long and how well the agent has known the applicant; an estimate of the applicant's net financial worth and annual income; the applicant's subsisting and pending insurance details. At times, the agent is also asked to submit a confidential report which helps the underwriter in effectively assessing the case and taking the right underwriting decision. The agent must also include critical details such as the family income of the client and his social status in his report.

Underwriters can take prompt decisions if complete information needed to make the evaluation of the insurance policy accompanies the application. The time needed to approve (at standard rates), reject, or load/rate (charge higher/substandard premium rates) the application can take a long

* The agent has been referred to as 'he' in this book for sake of simplicity. It means any person related to the context male or female.

time if the information available is incomplete. In these cases additional forms and questionnaires will be needed to be asked for. It is also an agent's duty to make sure that all relevant supporting documents for the underwriting decision-making process is appended to the application in the first instance. The importance of agent's communication with the underwriter should not be underestimated. Underwriters tend to take conservative stance on insurance risk aspects of each applicant. An agent who provides full, relevant, accurate and precise information about the risk as well as the positive aspects of an applicant may enable the underwriter to arrive at an informed objective underwriting decision.

The agent is usually the only person connected with the company who sees the client face-to-face and is best placed to make a fair visual health assessment. If there is anything unusual about the applicant that would require explanation, it is incumbent on the agent to convey that information to the insurance company; for example, obesity or a noticeable disability. Similarly in non-medical information an agent must take note and convey to the underwriter if the applicant's income is unusually low for his occupation or if he has additional sources of income to justify the proposed insurance sum; for example, a cleric may be making additional money through his business as a free lance writer. A good agent should include such related information with the report that accompanies the life insurance application to facilitate the underwriting process.

Box 2.4

Information Usually asked for in an Agent's Report or Declaration

- How long have you known the client?
- How well do you know the client?
- What do you estimate is the client's income/net worth?
- What is the applicant's life insurance policy in force?
- Is there any other application of the applicant pending for coverage?

The Doctor

The Medical Examination Report/Medical Examination (MER/ME) and Medical Tests

Medical examination is a part of life insurance process particularly if the age and the sum to be assured is higher than a specified limit. These limits are generally the same across the industry. However, minor variations may be there differing from company to company. For example, a company may require no medical tests for a client aged 30 applying for Rs. 25 lacs of life insurance policy but a 40 year old applying for the same policy sum assured may require a ME and some blood tests.

Companies generally publish and update these guidelines periodically and agents must remain abreast with these guidelines before completing the insurance policy forms and scheduling medical tests for their clients. An example of a model guideline for medical requirements is given in Annexure 3. If the client goes for a medical examination the doctor who examines the client fills in the MER.[6] Insurance companies have a contract with selected doctors and diagnostic centers in most of the cities for the purpose of conducting medical tests. These doctors and diagnostic centers are accountable for correct, fair and accurate assessment of the tests. Expenses on these tests etc. are paid for by the insurance companies. The contract of these testing agencies with the insurance companies does not allow them to share the results of the medical examinations and tests with the applicant. They are also not supposed to advise or administer treatment to the applicant while he is visiting them for the purpose of the insurance medical examination or tests.

It is important that the doctor first establishes the identity of the client by an identification document which the client has to supply to the doctor/medical centre. The medical report that the doctors send to the insurance company consists of two parts. The first part contains the questions broadly related to medical history in the application form, the only difference between the medical history in the application form and the one in the medical report form is that here the doctor is supposed to put the questions to the applicant and fill in the answers himself exactly as given by the applicant.

The second part consists of the physical examination. The physical examination starts with measurement of height and recording of weight. The doctor is also asked to indicate whether the applicant looks older than his stated age. The information regarding client's smoking and drinking habits are elicited and recorded. The blood pressure and the pulse reading have also to be recorded. The examining doctor has to examine and comment specifically regarding any abnormalities of the applicant's arteries/veins, heart, respiratory system, nervous system, abdomen, genitorinary system, ears, eyes, and skin. The doctor also reports the urinalysis result. As the sum assured increases the MER is supplemented by tests such as Electro Cardiograph (ECG), Fasting Blood Sugar (FBS), Chest X-ray, Blood chemistry and HIV and Hepatitis tests. The medical report is the property of the insurance company and is kept in confidence of the company.

Family Doctor/Attending Doctor's Report

Family Doctors are a source of information on applicants who have undergone medical treatment prior to applying for life insurance policies. Sometimes the information in the attending physician's files might influence the insurance company's underwriting decision. The underwriters specifically ask for the report from such doctors. However, there is mostly a delay in getting these reports which prolongs the duration of the underwriting process. To expedite the physician's response, whenever a client has had any treatment for an illness in the past, it is useful if agents requisition and send the personal medical reports of the client from the concerned doctors along with the life insurance application.

Verification

For plausible and proper functioning of the mechanism of life insurance, each applicant has to pay appropriate premium for the risk he brings to the insurance pool. This premium is decided based on the risk factors of the applicant mentioned by him in the application forms. The insurance law recognizes that many of these factors cannot be correctly known to the underwriters unless these are honestly and accurately mentioned by the applicant. The law, therefore imposes a duty on the applicant to make full disclosure of all material facts[7] in the application form. This is called the duty of 'uberrimae fides' or utmost good faith. The law states that in the event of failure to disclose material facts the insurance policy is considered void ab initio.[8]

Though the applicant is obligated to state the truth in the application and material misrepresentation[9] with intent to defraud can result in the claim being repudiated.[10] However, for high sum cases the company does not want to rely on the applicant's statement because even if the claim is denied due to misrepresentation and non disclosure, a substantial sum of money would already have been spent on medical tests, underwriting and agent commissions. Also to protect policy holders interests the law imposes an incontestability clause,[11] which stipulates that a claim cannot be rejected on grounds on non disclosure if it has been in-force for a stipulated period of time. Therefore, to limit the frauds and non disclosures by the applicants some insurance companies have instituted a system of random verification.

Random verification does to a great extent help to keep a check on fraudulent practices. It also helps in cross-checking of the authenticity of information given in the application form as well as the medical reports. Verification can be done through enquiries by insurance company staff or through the services of an independent verification agency. The unique advantage of these investigations is that they provide an evaluation of the application by an independent source having no interest in the outcome of the application. The degree and extent of thoroughness required in the investigation are linked to the sum of life insurance applied for. When the amount of insurance is small, the report may be brief, commenting in a general way on the applicant's health, habits, finances, environment and reputation. When the amount applied for is large, the verification report must be detailed with focus on the applicant's finances and personal ethics. The report calls for attention to applicant's financial adversities and it comments on the applicant's use of alcohol, tobacco, and other abnormal social indulgences. The verification should also bring out medical impairments if noticed in cases of non disclosures as such details could have been missed out by the medical examiner.

The information received as a result of the verification process about the applicant is matched with the information in the application form; in case of discrepancy the policy is not issued. In case the policy is issued by the time the verification report is received the company cancels the policy and declares it null and void.

UNDERWRITING PROCESS FLOW

The complete risk evaluation process has to be managed through a structured underwriting process flow to maintain efficiency and speed in decision-making. The underwriting department follows a step by step process flow to ensure that applicants and agents are advised of the result of the underwriting decision on a given schedule. This ensures good customer service and is also important for regulatory compliance which states that applicants should be informed of the status of their application within 15 days of the receipt of the application by the insurance company.[12]

The underwriting process flow can be divided into two parts, i.e. medical and non-medical. The underwriting starts when the underwriter receives the 'case' with the application form and other documents which are required as per the insurance company's guidelines. This may include identification documents, supplementary questionnaires, etc. In case the application is a 'medical case' then the underwriter reviews the case only after complete medical reports are received.

The life insurance cases are assigned to the underwriters on files or through an electronic data processing system. Applications and other documents can be scanned and distributed online to underwriters if the company has a computerized infrastructure. Otherwise, document files are assigned to underwriters when all required information is complete. The underwriter reviews the case and assesses it. In

DIAGRAM 2.1

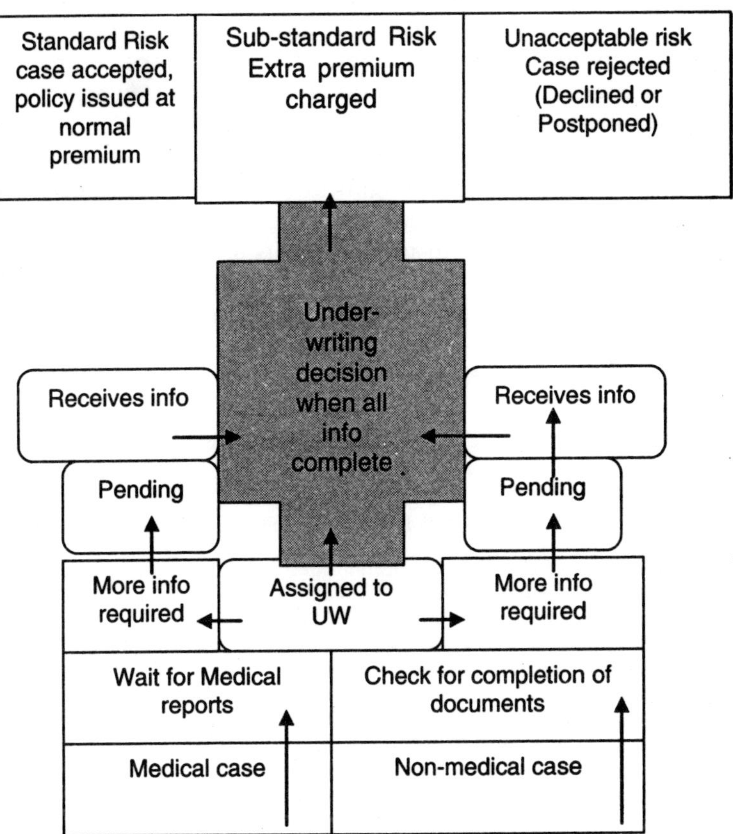

case the requirement of additional information the case is posted to the 'pending drawer'. This must be followed by a letter sent out either electronically or manually informing the client of the additional information/document requirements. In case all information is complete the agent and the customer are informed accordingly through a letter. In case the underwriter finds the risk factors of the case as average then the case is a standard risk case and the policy is issued.

If the underwriter finds that the risk in the case is higher than average the case is marked substandard and an additional premium is charged. In case the underwriter finds the risk unacceptable the case may be rejected either temporarily through postponement or permanently by declining.

In life insurance business the underwriting process is the key process to protect the interest of the insurance companies while being fair to the clients. It is an impersonalized activity in an intensely personalized field like life insurance. The success and efficiency of the underwriting process, however, depends on the promptness and thoroughness of the life insurance agents in their documentation and reporting skills. It is, therefore, imperative that the life insurance agents and the underwriting staff work as a team and observe the whole gamut of life insurance ethics with a sense of promptness and propriety.

Notes and References

1. Sum Assured is the amount to be paid out when the policy matures or on earlier (death) claim, provided that premiums have been paid in full.
2. An agent is a licensed life insurance company representative who solicits contracts of insurance and provides service to the policyholder for the insurer.
3. A sample life insurance application form is given in Annexure 4.
4. Family members include parents, siblings and spouse.
5. According to the IRDA Protection of Policyholders Interest Regulations, 2002, the insurer or its agent shall ensure that the proposal form is filled in by the applicant. Where he is not able to fill in the form personally either because of inability to understand the language or inability to read and write, the applicant may secure the help of a person other than an insurance agent or employee or other intermediary to fill in the proposal form on his behalf. In such cases the proposal form shall contain a declaration to the effect that the contents of the proposal form have been explained to the applicant and have been fully understood by him and replies have been recorded as per the information provided by the applicant and the answers have been read out to and fully understood by and confirmed by the applicant and the said declaration shall be signed by the person who filled in the proposal form on behalf of the applicant.
6. A sample Medical Examination Report (MER) is given in Annexure 5.
7. Material fact is a fact of such importance that were it revealed in an insurance application, the underwriting decision would have been different.
8. To void a policy *ab initio* is to invalidate it from the beginning.
9. Material misrepresentation is a misrepresentation that would effect the insurance company's evaluation of the applicant.
10. Repudiating a claim is rejecting it by not paying out the insurance benefit amount.
11. Incontestability clause in the policy provides that the insurance company shall not be able to contest the statements in the application in the

application form if the policy has been in effect for a given length of time (two or three years) unless the insurance company can prove that the statement was made with fraudulent intention and the insured knew at the time of making the statement that it was false. If an insured lied as to the conditions of his health at the time of the policy was applied for, that lie cannot be used to contest payment under the policy if death occurred after the time limit stated in the incontestable clause. The key legislation governing insurance in India, the 'Insurance Act, 1938' outlines this clause in Section 45.

12. Annexure 7 contains the Insurance Regulatory and Development Authority (Protection of Policyholders' Interests) Regulations, 2002.

PART II

NON-MEDICAL, FINANCIAL AND MEDICAL UNDERWRITING

Chapter 3

Non-Medical Underwriting

Learning Objectives

The material in this chapter should enable the reader to understand

- Non-medical insurance meaning and concept
- Safeguards used by the companies for non-medical risks
- Disadvantages and advantages of non-medical insurance
- Non-medical factors evaluated for underwriting assessment
- Underwriting ratings for occupational, avocational and residential risks

CHAPTER

3

Non-Medical Underwriting

NON-MEDICAL INSURANCE

A substantial portion of new life insurance policies are underwritten without medical examination. All applicants for life insurance policies are not required to undergo medical examination and tests. This practice started in UK in the early twentieth century and in its early days it was limited to young applicants applying for small sums of insurance. When claims experience was seen to be favorable over the years, this practice became the norm in all life insurance companies for wider ranges of age and sum assured. Limited amount of medical information related to the applicant's medical history, family medical history and tobacco or alcohol use, however, is required in non-medical cases also.[1]

The potential risk of the likely non-disclosure of basic medical information does exist in non-medical cases. The underwriter has to mostly rely on statements made by the applicant as there is no other device to verify the statement of the applicant about his own helath. In the absence of medical examination and laboratory tests many health conditions may not come to light. Diseases which can occur without overt symptoms such as diabetes or hypertension may remain undisclosed as either the applicant may not know that they suffer from these diseases, or they intentionally hide the fact. Therefore, to minimize the increased risk of non disclosures of the diseases the life insurance companies have evolved certain safeguards which are in place for non-medical cases.

Box 3.1

Non-medical Life Insurance = No medical tests for applicants applying for a small sum assured/death benefit at younger ages unless any adverse medical information is disclosed in the application form.

NON-MEDICAL INSURANCE SAFEGUARDS

Limiting the Sum Assured and the Age for Non-medical Applicants (Non-medical Limits)

The most important safeguard that the companies use is limiting the allowed sum of life insurance to clients. In the early days of liberalization of the insurance sector in India the new players entering the market allowed non-medical insurance only up to Rs. 6 to 8 lacs of death benefit for clients with ages less than 35 years. When the claims experience of the companies turned out to be lower than was expected, the limits were gradually raised. Today, most companies provide up to Rs. 10 lacs on a non-medical basis for ages less than 35 years.[2] The policies that can be allowed without medical examinations reduce as the age goes up and insurance amount increases. Previous policies that have been taken from the company are added up to the present amount applied, in order to calculate whether the sum assured falls in the non-medical limit.

Box 3.2

How is Medical/Non-medical Limit Devised?

A study of claims received by insurance company found that the extra mortality due to impairments which were concealed or not known by the non-medical applicants and could have been found by a medical examination resulted in cost of Rs. 0.75 per Rs. 1000 of sum assured for ages below 30. The expense of medical examination in case of each applicant is Rs. 100. Thus 100/0.75 is the ratio of expense over cost. This ratio when multiplied with Rs. 1000 comes to approximately 133,000. Thus for applicants below the age of 30 applying for life insurance, a sum assured of up to Rs. 133,000 will be cost effective and can be safely categorized as non-medical.

Converting a Non-medical Application into a Medical if the case is a Substandard Risk

Another safeguard to reduce risk of non disclosure in non-medical cases is limiting the issue of non-medical life insurance only to standard risks.

If the client mentions any illness or symptoms of disease in the application form, the underwriter calls for relevant medical tests. Applicants in risk prone occupations like those working in mining or chemical industries may also be sent for medical

Box 3.3

Medical Tests are requested if in a non-medical case the client states the following conditions in the application form

Condition Stated	*Miners and chemical industry workers' Medical Tests that the Underwriter can ask for*
Family history of heart disease/ diabetes/stroke in more than 2 family members (family members include parents, siblings and spouse)	Medical Examination report (MER), Fasting Blood Sugar (FBS)
Death of family members due to above	MER, FBS
Diseases before 60 years of age.	MER, FBS, Electrocardiograph (ECG)
Overweight client	MER, FBS, ECG
Heavy smokers (more than 10 cigarettes a day)	MER, FBS and Liver Function Tests (LFT)
Heavy drinkers (more than 50 ml of hard drinks a day)	MER or/and other relevant tests that the underwriter thinks necessary
Any disclosed medical problem in the form other than minor illnesses	MER, Chest X-Ray or/and other relevant tests that underwriter thinks necessary

tests. Such tests are also asked for applicants in such occupations which involve exposure to harmful and noxious substances for substantial periods of time which can give rise to respiratory problems. The underwriters ask for a medical test to evaluate the health risks before taking a decision on such a case.

Mandating Identification (ID) Proofs

Unlike western countries, in India there is no standard identification number or document available for all citizens. Life insurance companies provide a list of acceptable identification proofs, which are mandatory requirements for all insurance application irrespective of the age of the applicant or sum of life insurance. The name and age of the client on the ID proof submitted must match what is stated in the application form. To prevent fraud the underwriters always examine the ID proof for any signs of tampering or forgery.

Strict Parameters for Non-medical Automatic/ Computerized Underwriting

To speed up the process of issuance of non-medical cases, the details of the application are entered into a computer program and the computer program, based on pre-defined parameters, either issues the policy or in case of any parameter inadequacy sends the case to an underwriter for review. In companies where non-medical underwriting is automated and the computer takes a decision instead of the underwriters, the parameters set for issuing a policy are very stringent. Only non-medical cases, with small sum assured and without any adverse factors recorded in the application form pass through to policy issue. Thus even though the computerized underwriting speeds up the process for the issue of life insurance policies of non-medical standard cases it does not compromise on the risk element.

Limiting Insurance on Juvenile (Children) Lives

Life insurance companies not only limit life insurance for non-medical cases based on age and sum assured but they also put limits on the life insurance of children. Life insurance as a financial device protects the income of dependants in case the earning member dies. Since children are not earning members in a family and are themselves dependant on others there does not exist any need for risk coverage through life insurance. The life insurance policy sold to children, is therefore, purely for investment reasons. Consequently, certain insurance products such as term insurance[3] are not sold to children.

To avoid misuse of life insurance cover on children, applications for life insurance on children are very carefully underwritten. The underwriters cope with the situation in issuing juvenile policies in two ways: (1) by limiting the coverage to amounts much smaller than those available to adults, particularly for very young children, and (2) by verifying that the life insurance on the children equals the life insurance in force on the other members of the family, especially the breadwinner. This is a good index to ensure the bonafides of the purpose of the child insurance as also to eliminate any chance of malafide intentions.

Life insurance companies are eager to sell policies to children as they find juvenile cases profitable due to relatively lesser mortality risk. With the exception of the first few weeks after birth, the death rate is very low amongst the children and does not begin to climb until around the age of 10. The death rate is high immediately after birth because of the hazards of natal environment, congenital defects and the delicate physical resistance of a newborn. This period of heavy mortality is avoided by limiting coverage to children who have attained the age of 1 month, 3 months, or 6 months. Family economics and the social strata of the family have great influence on the mortality of a child. This makes it important to inquire about the family income etc. Medical tests are usually not required in such cases except for high sums assured. However, rules differ from company to company. Usually only healthy juveniles are issued life insurance policies. Health problems reflected in the application form are investigated thoroughly before issue of the policy. Some insurance companies however, do not issue policies to medically substandard children.

ADVANTAGES AND DISADVANTAGES OF NON-MEDICAL INSURANCE FOR THE LIFE INSURANCE COMPANIES

Majority of applications in life insurance companies are non-medical. While companies are particular about evaluation of each and every risk factor as discussed earlier is it not surprising that in their overall business interest they let most of the applications get through without medical examinations. Life insurance companies do most of their business through non-medical route because there are many advantages of non-medical life insurance.

Advantages

Non-medical cases can be processed faster, hassles of medical examinations get eliminated and there is no delay in issue of policies. It removes one of the greatest psychological barriers for a customer, which is of facing doctors for the purchase of life insurance policies. Also when comparing the extra mortality rate of non-medical and medical policies the disparity between non-medical and medical mortality at young ages is reasonably low. The mortality disparities increase as the age of clients increases. Thus the rationale for non-medical insurance is that at ages under 30, the rate of mortality is low and the probability of finding medical problems on examination is very low. Life insurance companies set their non-medical limits on the basis of their own experiences and expense assumptions on clients' mortality. Non-medical limits of various life insurance companies may also differ in response to competitive factors of the market.

Disadvantages

The life insurance companies do have certain safeguard which have been discussed earlier but non-medical insurance still has a slightly higher rate of mortality than medically examined business. This extra mortality comes from (1) impairments known to the applicant but deliberately concealed, and (2) impairments not known to the applicant that could have been discovered by a medical examination.

Box 3.4

An Equation
Non-medical business is profitable only till
Cost of claims < Cost of medical examinations/tests

NON-MEDICAL FACTORS EVALUATED FOR RISK

Life insurance companies seek detailed information in the application forms to evaluate the non-medical cases and categorize them methodically in proper risk categories. These significant non-medical factors for risk assessment are as follows:

- age
- gender
- personal history
- habits
- morals
- family history
- avocation
- occupation
- residence
- economic status
- plan of insurance

Age

Mortality tables clearly reflect the age of the client as the single most important factor for mortality expectations. An individual's resistance to disease and injury attenuates as the age advances and the body grows older. Since the risk increases with the increase in age the insurance companies charge higher premiums. Companies do not issue insurance policies after a certain age as the risk becomes very high and the applicants become uninsurable. Most insurance products have a maximum entry age of 60 years. Some may have lower or higher ages depending on the design of the product. Whole life plans[4] may allow individuals to apply till the age of 70 while certain accident or critical illness riders[5] may restrict the entry age to 50 or 55 years.[5]

The age of the applicant is of great importance and needs to be proved by relevant documents. The age proof also serves as the identity proof of the applicant. The signature and date of birth stated on the identification document is cross-checked with that given on the application form. Cases do come to light when an incorrect statement of age is discovered after the policy has been issued; in such cases the sum of the proceeds is reduced in accordance with the misstatement-of-age clause.[6]

Acceptable Date of Birth Proofs (Identification Documents)

- Passport
- Driving License
- PAN Card
- Ration Card
- Voter's Identity Card
- High School or equivalent Certificate
- Employer's Certificate (Government and Public Sector Employees)

Not Acceptable Date of Birth Proofs

- Affidavits
- Self-declaration
- School Leaving Certificate

Box 3.5

> Some companies treat the non acceptable date of birth proofs as a risk factor and add an extra amount to the standard premium (Rs. 2 per 1000 of sum assured is added to the premium) for clients who do not have acceptable proof of date of birth. They thus classify such applicants as a substandard case.

Gender

The life span of women is longer than men and generally they have lower mortality rates. Especially in late teens and early twenties male mortality is much higher than female mortality. However, there is an increased risk associated with women due to their unfavorable socio economic status in India. Cases of dowry deaths and even culpable homicide (like bride burning) are occasionally reported. Therefore, underwriting of life insurance policies for women applicants is stringent if they are not well educated or are not earning members of the family either as salaried employee, self-employed or professionals.

Professional, salaried, wage earning and income generating women are treated at par with men for life insurance purposes. Life insured sum allowed for such women depends on the income of the applicant woman. Housewives, unemployed and unmarried dependant women are generally allowed very small life insurance sum and that too only if other family members are insured. Women who have passive income through rentals or investments are also allowed only small amount of life insurance coverage. Women are not eligible term plans if they are non-earning and dependant housewives.

Personal History

Previous Insurance

Personal history includes the details about the applicant's health, his habits related to tobacco and alcohol use and details of life insurance policies taken earlier. The applicant's previous life insurance is taken into account to calculate the total insurance sum to be allowed based on his income. The underwriter must judge whether the sum of insurance, present and applied for bears a reasonable relationship to the applicant's needs and financial resources. The life insurance need is taken into account based on all existing and applied for insurance policies on the client's life.

If there is no previous insurance and the applicant is applying for a large sum at an advanced age the underwriter must consider this as a 'be cautious' signal. The underlying suspicion being that the applicant has been prompted by ill health or financial crisis to take high value life insurance policy. The risk thus increases for the life insurance company and the underwriter must ask for further documents and details to clear all possible doubts about the client. The insurance companies also demand to know whether the applicant has ever been refused life insurance coverage by any other insurance company or offered life insurance on rated (substandard risk) terms. A previously rated applicant would need to be investigated for the specific medical condition which might have become worse over a period of time.

Adverse Medical History

The applicant's health record consists of information about his previous illnesses, injuries and surgical operations. Past adverse medical history of a serious nature would prompt the underwriters to request for special/additional medical tests or examinations. In such cases even the personal doctor of the applicant may need to be contacted for requisite medical details.

Family Medical History

The life insurance application forms contain questions about family history. Answers to these questions provide information about the ages and state of health of parents and brothers and sisters of the applicant whether living or deceased. Details of their ages at death and the causes of death are also required. Family history is considered significant because certain health and medical characteristics are usually hereditary. Maladies such as coronary heart disease, diabetes, high blood pressure are known to be hereditary. A good family medical history with long life span of parents and siblings enjoying good health are considered as 'positives' by the underwriters. Such positives sometimes do outweigh certain negative factors such as marginal overweight conditions. On the contrary a adverse family medical history may attract substandard premium rates more so if the applicant also has other negative risk factors.

Even though underwriters give quite some importance to family medical history it is not an absolutely reliable source of information to base the underwriting decisions. For example the family members may not know the exact causes of ill-health or death of their kin. Also a tendency exists amongst the applicants to exaggerate the longevity of deceased family members. It is also common for many applicants to generally report their family members in good health; unless they are either dead or suffering from some serious illness. Instances of hypertension, diabetes and other such impairments which are regarded as significant medical risks by underwriters are at times not disclosed by the applicants. There is yet another problem which is found in reviewing the family history in life insurance application forms. It is not feasible to trace the applicant's preceding generation's medical records. While only data concerning the applicant's parents and siblings are usually required in application forms the hereditary characteristics may manifest from grandparents and great-grandparents.

The assessment of true impact of heredity on longevity is difficult. Gathering pertinent information that can be used to accurately measure the hereditary influences on longevity and health of an applicant is also not easy. Despite all these problems family history remains an important part of the insurance applications and underwriters still co-relate it with other health factors to determine the possible future health conditions and the longevity of applicants. In fact experienced underwriters do not use family history solely to rate up the premiums. The underwriter may chose to ignore family history of diabetes in one or both parents but will rate the case if applicant's father and mother had diabetes and the applicant also smokes, is overweight and has high cholesterol. The totality of risk factors is important for underwriter for correct risk classification. The probability of some diseases is increased if the parents or family members have suffered from it. These diseases are hereditary and can transcend from generation to generation. Some of the diseases which are passed down the generations and considered significant by the underwriters are:

- Diabetes
- Heart disease and Stroke
- Ovarian, breast and colon cancer
- Thallasemia and haemophilia-blood disorders

THE UNDERWRITER'S CHECKLIST

Underwriters typically ask themselves the following questions:

- How many family members have/had the disease (one parent, both parents, siblings)?
- What age did they have the disease? (an early age onset of disease is regarded more serious)?
- Whether they died or survived the disease?

Occupational Hazards

The International Labor organization has estimated the annual figure for work related deaths as 1.1 million people globally. Accidents represent only 30% of the total mortality while diseases account for the rest.[7] Insurance companies, therefore, have to charge for the extra risk on applicants engaged in certain occupations which entail higher than average risks. All life insurance companies have occupational hazard manuals in which they list the occupations that are deemed to have adverse effects on life spans and health. A client employed in one of the listed occupations is required to pay additional premium, even if all medical parameters and other factors are favorable. Underwriting guidelines include questionnaires for a list of occupations. These carry relevant questions on risky activities. These forms have to be completed whenever an applicant states that he is working in any of the listed occupations. The higher mortality rates associated with these occupations may be due to a greater than normal accident hazard or unhealthy working conditions or adverse effect on the body system and thus increasing the incidence of disease.

Accident Hazards

Accidents are common hazards in many occupations. All people working on machines and other heavy equipments are exposed to variable degrees of accident hazards. Construction workers may fall victim to a plunge or may be seriously hit during the construction activities. Miners have the risk of mine's caving in, explosions, rock falls and fire. Electrical workers may be exposed to electrocution by high electricity voltages or some to the danger of falling from high poles/transformers/pylons. Laborers handling heavy materials run the risk of having the materials fall on them. Fishermen may face the risk of tidal waves and other perils of the sea. Police, military and para-military personnel have the risk of being injured or killed in riots, rescue missions, terrorist attacks, insurgencies or wars.

Dusts and Poisonous Gases

Persons working in certain industries are exposed to dusts and poisonous gases produced by the operations processes such as grinding, drilling, etc. Contaminants such as silica, metal, textile or wool fibers can cause respiratory problems which adversely affect the life span of individuals. The lasting effects of exposures to dust during employment in such trades, is an important underwriting factor to take note of. Exposure to asbestos is also a proven serious health hazard. Different forms of poison are used in many industries as raw material for making various products. Exposure to lead has largely been associated with the mining and smelting of lead. Lead exposure is also associated with printing, painting and file-cutting. These occupational hazards are major risk factors that underwriters take due note of.

Socio-economic Hazards

Unskilled and semi-skilled jobs employing labor at low wages are associated with extra mortality risks due to unsatisfactory living and working conditions and non-availability of adequate medical care. Low economic status of such laborers adversely impacts their substandard physical and mental capacity. There are other occupations which have socio-economic hazards not because of low income but because of the environment in which the employees work. Bartenders, liquor vendors, and cab/bus/truck drivers, for example, are known to be prone to health hazards purely due to their working environment which exposes them to smoking, drug addiction and alcohol abuse.

Usually underwriters link their decisions only to the current occupation of the applicant. If an applicant is placed in a substandard risk classification because of an unfavorable current occupation, on change to a favorable occupation, his rating is usually removed and the premium is relevantly reduced. In some cases previous employment in a hazardous occupation may be the basis for a substandard underwriting. This can happen when there is reason to believe that the applicant may return to the previous occupation or a health problem caused by the previous occupation has already manifested.

Common Occupations that Affect Underwriting Decisions[8]

Indicative decisions such as standard, substandard or declined for a few occupations are given below. In case a particular occupation or service is substandard, the ratings (extra premium) are expressed in a 'per mille flat extra' which is the increase per Rs. 1000 of sum assured such as Rs. 2 pm or Rs. 3 pm. The rating for accident riders is typically expressed as multiples known as 'multiplier' for example 2x or 4x.[9]

Pilots

In the early days of aviation flying was a hazardous profession. In those days life insurance companies did not cover the risk of death or injury in any form of aviation. In cases where it was covered it was subject to a substantial extra premium. With technical advancements and state of the art planes the hazards of flying have considerably reduced. The underwriting restrictions consequently have also been relaxed. Today, the life risk on account of flying has been brought to a very low level. Air travel has become so common that life insurance companies do not consider it necessary to impose any underwriting restrictions on either pilots or passengers travel on any type of non-military aircraft. There is no occupational rating (extra premium) or restriction on pilots or crew members flying on regularly scheduled commercial aircrafts. The rating on pilots of private planes, which fly on unscheduled routes depends on the pilot's age, experience, training, and frequency of flying.

Rating for pilots of military aircrafts is dependent on the type of aircraft he flies. Pilot's age and type of flying missions are also taken into account. Applicants flying any type of plane are usually required to complete a supplementary form (aviation questionnaire). These forms contain the full details of the aircraft owning company's past, present, and probable future aviation activities. The form usually asks questions about type of aircraft being flown including its make and the owners of the aircraft. Other details required to be disclosed by pilots applying for life insurance are as follows:

- The number of years since flying,
- Training level, and
- Number of hours flown in the past year and if there was any private flying on unscheduled routes.

Rating

- *Pilots of Commercial Airlines*: Standard,
- *Other Aircrafts* (private, chartered planes, etc.): Depends on the type of plane the applicant flies, and
- *Air force Pilots (Fighter Planes)*: Maybe declined life insurance cover.

Military and Police Personnel

Service in the Army is regarded as a high risk job. A very conservative view is taken of such cases especially if the client is in the border areas. The branches of army which include paratroopers, divers, infantry, engineers, artillery and army/navy/air-force special task force personnel are also considered as serious life risks. The underwriters make an assessment of the type of risk which the particular branch exposes the client to. There are some branches in the armed forces such as anti-terrorist sqauds, special action commandos, bomb disposal squads and Para-troopers which are at higher risks than other army, navy or air-force personnel. Such applicants may be declined life insurance or charged a given higher extra premium. In case of naval personnel the risk is assessed differently. Baring submarine personnel and naval divers the naval occupation is considered less risky than army. Air force engineers and administrative personnel are put in the standard category while rating of pilots depends on whether they fly fighter planes or transport planes. Police personnel have lower risks than army personnel provided they are not involved in counter terrorist or commando or bomb disposal operations.

Ratings

- Armed forces/BSF personnel:
  Life cover: 2 per mille
  Accident Rider: may be declined
- Police force:
  Life: Standard
  Accident Rider: 2x (if not involved in commando or bomb disposal, etc.)

Mining and Refineries

There is a considerable risk involved for people working in mines and oil refineries. The risk here is substantially dependent on the position and type of work a person performs. Usually geologists and engineers have much less risk than skilled or semi skilled workers at the site. The risk is mainly due to high incidence of accidents. Also the nature of work or exposure to hazardous inhalants may affect the health of the workers which may cause long-term chronic health problems. India has less stringent work place safety regulations than the developed countries. Inadequate compliance to work place safety norms is also rampant in India. Therefore, the underwriters usually tend to view workplace hazards of these occupations seriously and rate these occupations conservatively. Extra loading is dependent on the workplace, hierarchical designation, type of industry and the applicant's job profile. For some occupations the underwriters may offer the life insurance cover as standard but charge the accident rider, if applicable, at substandard rates.

Ratings

1. For Mining Industry

Low Risk Occupations: Include engineers, geologist, white collar employees etc.
Life cover: standard
Accident Rider: Rider 2x

High Risk Occupations: Include firemen, Foremen, Shafts men, Cutters, Clippers, etc.
Life cover: 2 per mille
Accident Rider: decline

2. Oil and Natural Gas Companies

Low Risk Occupations: Include geologist, clerical staff, surveyors, office staff, etc.
Life cover: Standard
Accident Rider: 2x

Intermediate Risk Occupations: Include Marine installation personnel, Superintendents, Engineers, etc.
Life cover: 1 per mille
Accident Rider: 3x

High Risk Occupations: Include welders, rig mechanics, etc.
Life cover: 2 per mille
Accident Rider: decline

Merchant Navy

Merchant navy personnel are exposed to accident risks. Merchant Navy sailor's premium depends on their rank and the type of ship they are sailing on. Oil carrying ships are considered riskier than cargo ships. General principle to be followed in risk rating her is, higher the rank, lower the risk. Mostly merchant navy personnel fall in the range of intermediate to low risks in general.

Other Occupations

Drivers: Drivers fall in either intermediate or low risk category based on the type of vehicle a driver drives. For example truck drivers may be put in sub standard category but taxi drivers can be taken as standard risks.

Construction Workers: Risk category of construction workers will vary according to the nature of job they perform and their nature of work deployment. Generally they fall in high to intermediate grades of risk.

Avocation

Nature of certain hobbies that people indulge in is quite hazardous. Such hobbies attract extra premium. Racing (car, motorbike, speed boat, etc.); sky diving; scuba diving; and mountaineering may attract extra premium. Depending on the risks associated with a particular hobby or sport, risk prone avocations have a flat extra rating of Rs. 2.00 to Rs. 10.00 per Rs. 1,000 of sum assured.

Travels and Residence

Geographical factors also have major impact on life expectancy. Mortality rates do vary according to geographical regions. This holds good within India as also other parts of the world. Where a person lives and works does make a difference to his life expectancy. Issues inherent in the underwriting decisions include applicant's residential locations and also foreign travel. This is an accepted determinant of risk. Poor medical facilities, extreme climate and difficult topography have real implications in the event of a medical emergency. HIV and AIDs are spreading at epidemic proportion in many countries. In sub-Saharan Africa, where life expectancies are already low, life expectancy has dropped to 40 years or less due to HIV and AIDs.

Political and economic conditions of a country are also important issues both from the point of view of mortality and from the perspective of the business cost to life insurance operations. In countries, where there is rampant corruption at national and local levels, it may be easy and inexpensive to obtain fake death certificates and autopsy records. Considerable time and expense are associated with investigating a death claim from a foreign country. These are additional reasons which make residence an important factor in assessing the risk of the client. For applicants who live or travel extensively to certain underdeveloped countries such as those in Africa or Latin America the insurance companies decide on the premium based on which category the concerned country falls in the underwriting manual.[10]

While residents in some of the African countries are declined life insurance altogether, in some other they are charged extra premium. This depends on the level of crime, social law and order, war and diseases prevalent in those countries. For some countries there is no clear cut policy and the case is decided on the occupational background, profile, exact city or location of residence in their respective country and income of the applicant.

Details of flat extra premiums which life insurance companies may charge for a resident in under-developed countries is given below.

Country-Decision	*Country-Decision*	*Country-Decisión*	*Country-Decision*
Africa	**Asia**	**Europe**	**Americas**
Congo—Decline	Afghanistan—Decline	Bulgaria—3 pm	Brazil—1 pm
Kenya—Decline	Bangladesh—4 pm	Croatia—3 pm	Argentina—1 pm
Nigeria—Decline	Lebanon—4 pm	Uzbekistan—3 pm	America—Std
Ghana—4 pm	Indonesia—2 pm	Ukraine—3 pm	Canada—Std
Namibia—2 pm	Saudi Arabia—2 pm	Yugoslavia—IC	US—Std
South Africa—IC	SriLanka—IC	Serbia—IC	Mexico—Std
Tanzania—IC	China—IC	Kosovo—IC	Trinidad—Std
Sudan—Decline	Kuwait—IC	UK—Std	
Somalia—Decline	Pakistan—IC	France—Std	
Uganda—Decline	Qatar—Std	Germany—Std	
	UAE—Std		
	Oman—Std		
	Singapore—Std		
	Thailand—Std		
	Japan—Std		
	New Zealand—Std		
	Australia—Std		

IC — Individual Consideration on a case to case basis,
Std — Standard, pm — per mil

Insurance for NRIs and Foreign Nationals

Insurance is given to Non-Resident Indians (NRI) but they have to be present in the country during the time of taking a life insurance policy. Further a NRI taking a life insurance policy must sign the application in India and the premium is paid in Indian Rupees (INR). If an Indian life insurance company has an office in a foreign country, it can issue policies to people of Indian origin in that country and the premium can be paid in foreign currency. Persons from foreign countries residing in India on a permanent basis or for extended periods can be insured by Indian life insurance companies and there is no rule barring the insurance of such persons though the underwriter has to satisfy that all legal and risk requirements are settled before the life insurance policy is issued.

Habits and Morals

Habits

The term habits, for underwriting purpose, refers to the use of alcohol, tobacco, drug abuse or addiction to any other intoxicating material. The use of drugs leads to impairment of judgment and sluggish reactions during the intoxication. This increases the risk of accidents coupled with the effect on the individual's general state of health. Drug addicts are usually declined insurance. Further, there is a substantial relapse rate among the de-addicted drug abusers. Consequently a person who is known to be a drug addict cannot obtain insurance on basis of a de-addiction treatment certificate. Prolonged use of immoderate quantity of alcohol is also harmful to a person's health. Insurance companies are generally not averse to giving life insurance policy to an applicant who uses alcoholic beverages in moderate quantities on social occasions. A medical test is called for if the applicant discloses alcohol use that is higher than what can be considered occasional social drinking. All data available on the effect of drinking on longevity indicate that there is a substantial mortality increase amongst the heavy drinkers. Apart from the damage to life systems a high proclivity of accidents and suicides has also been reported amongst the life insurance policy-holders with history of alcoholism. Similarly heavy smokers are susceptible to many diseases and the insurance companies usually take a very conservative view even if of smokers claim to have left smoking. Details of ratings for smokers are discussed under medical underwriting in chapter 6.

Morals

Insurance companies definitely review the morals of the applicants. This is surprising to many people and may seem like an unnecessary intrusion into the applicant's personal life. Insurance companies get interested in the moral conduct of the client because it is known that persons with unethical or immoral conduct have an extra life risk compared to people who follow the social norms of ethics and morality. Behavior patterns which are considered immoral (such as unfaithfulness to spouse) are viewed seriously, partly because they are frequently found in combination with other types of risky behavior, such as over-indulgence in alcoholic beverages, gambling and the use of drugs and partly because such conduct gives rise to physical risks from others. Unethical business conduct also, if known, is taken into consideration while deciding the life insurance application. There is evidence to show that misrepresentation and concealment of material underwriting facts in the applications is linked to dishonest and unethical business. practices by applicants. In case a company which is applying for a key man insurance policy for its employee is found to be involved in any unethical business practices the underwriter should not issue him the life insurance policy. In such life insurance cases the insuring company may become the target of unscrupulous schemes.[11]

NOTES AND REFERENCES

1. Insurance Underwriting: A Managerial Perspective, Vol. III, 2002, ICFAI University Press.
2. Annexure 3 gives the medical and non-medical table for an insurance company in India.
3. Term life insurance is the original form of life insurance and is considered to be pure insurance protection because it builds no cash

value (The amount available in cash upon cancellation of an insurance policy). This is in contrast to life insurance products such as whole life, endowment and unit linked. Term life insurance is temporary, as it covers only a specific period of time, the relevant term. If the insured dies during the term, the death benefit will be paid to the beneficiary. If the term expires the insurer does not have to pay out making term insurance the most inexpensive way to purchase a substantial death benefit.

4. Whole life plan is a permanent type of life insurance coverage that combines a death benefit and accumulates a cash value. The face value is constant, and this amount will be paid if the insured person dies at any time while the coverage is in effect. Premium costs are unchanging and remain the same from the original date the policy goes into effect to the date of maturity. The policy is intended to mature at age 100—this is the age when premium payments would end and the cash value would equal the face value. At time of maturity, the face value would be paid to an insured person who is still living.
5. A rider is an add-on benefit available with an insurance plan. Accident riders provide coverage in the event of death due to accidental injuries, but not illness. Critical illness rider makes benefits payable to the insured for medical expenses prior to death and is paid upon diagnosis of the illness. While the illnesses covered and the premiums vary among insurers, most insurers cover cancer, coronary artery bypass, heart attack, kidney/renal failure, major organ transplant and paralytic stroke.
6. Misstatement of Age Clause provides that if misstatement of age is discovered after the policy is issued, the company can, if the insured is currently alive, adjust the premium amount on future premiums and request payment of any additional premium the policy owner should have paid; or if the insured has died, adjust the face amount of the policy to fit the premium that was paid at the correct age before paying the claim.
7. Takala, J., Occupational Safety and Health Branch, International Labor Organization, Geneva 1999.
8. Underwriting Guide for Financial Advisers including an Occupation and Sports & Pastimes Guide for Disability Benefits, Friends Provident.
9. Annexure 6 gives details on the Flat Extra Rating and Multiplier method and example of its use for calculating extra premium.
10. International Underwriting Challenges and Opportunities, Brad Gabel, CLU, FALU, FLMI, Vice-President and Chief Underwriter, AIG Life Brokerage
11. McGill's Life Insurance, Fifth Edition, Edward, E. Graves, Editor, Lynn Hayes, Managing Editor, The American College Press, 2004.

Chapter 4

Financial Underwriting

The material in this chapter should enable the reader to understand

- Financial Underwriting concepts and risks of over-insurance
- Financial Underwriting for individuals: Guidelines, Safeguards and Limitations
- Financial Underwriting for Business (Keyperson/ Partnership): Guidelines

CHAPTER

4

Financial Underwriting

CONCEPTS OF FINANCIAL UNDERWRITING

Financial underwriting, concept, is that area of underwriting which aims at ensuring that there is no error of over-insurance, no error of speculation and no scope for fraud arising out of pure monetary considerations on part of the beneficiaries. The main reason for purchasing a life insurance policy is to cater for the precariousness and the uncertainty of life. A buyer of life insurance policy wants to provide for his family, dependants and his business interests in case of his untimely death. However, the life insurance guarantees unfortunately sometimes may have an unethical and undesirable effect. It may tempt a beneficiary[1] to kill the insured person in order to obtain the proceeds of his life insurance policy. It may even tempt an insured person when facing a financial crisis to commit suicide in order to secure his family's future.

Financial underwriting, simply put, attempts to protect against this kind of malpractice by ensuring that the amount of life insurance is in accordance with the applicant's status, known legal assets and income. The factors used to determine the adequacy of the insurance amount are a combination of income, material net worth and insurable interest. If there is any evidence of potential fraud, malivalence or over-insurance, the application for life insurance must be denied/declined. There is no mechanism available with the underwriters to neutralize these factors. The underwriter cannot compensate for this risk by charging any extra premium as happens in the case of medical substandard risks.[2]

Financial underwriting is defined as "using the investigation and evaluation of the financial data on a risk under consideration in order to determine the acceptability of that risk for insurance coverage."[3] Financial indicators, such as income, profitability and liquidity provide the insurer with information to analyze the suitable amount of insurance and eliminate the 'moral hazard'. The basic questions which have to be answered in connection with financial underwriting are:

- *Appropriateness*—Is the application based on a valid, insurable interest?
- *Consistency*—Are the type of policy applied for and, in particular, the sum to be insured reasonable?
- *Affordability*—Are sufficient resources available with the applicant to enable payment of future premiums?

In financial underwriting, the first step in the underwriting process is to identify the type of cover. There are two key types of insurance covers, individual or personal cover (e.g. family protection, non-business loan protection, investment or savings) and business cover, (e.g. business loan protection, partnership protection or key person cover).[4]

The fundamental rule of financial underwriting is to never allow someone to be worth more dead than alive. Over-insurance (obtaining insurance in excess of what is proportionate to the loss of income an applicant's family suffers on demise of the insured person) has a potential to turn a life insurance policy into a case of murder, suicide or lapse.

Over-insurance fallouts

Murder

Cases of murder for insurance money have made news in western countries. In the United States several courts have evolved the concept of insurable interest and an insurer's duty to investigate the financial worth of the applicant before granting life insurance. It is a general rule in the United States that a murderer or his heirs should not be allowed to profit from their wrongful act by receiving any share of the victim's estate. The principle that no person shall be permitted to benefit from the consequences of his or her wrongdoing is applied to prevent murderers from gaining from their victims, whether through the route of inheritance, intestacy statute, or a life insurance policy. The concept of insurable interest which has been discussed earlier operates on the same principle. If negligent issuance of a policy or change of beneficiary results in the murder of, or injury to the insured by the beneficiary or someone acting on his behalf in an attempt to obtain the proceeds of the life insurance policy, the insuring company may incur legal liability and can be sued for adjudication by the relevant court of law.[5]

Box 4.1

The landmark judgment in *Overstreet v. Kentucky Central Life Insurance Company case*, the beneficiary was convicted of procuring the insured's murder. In holding that the insured's estate had a cause of action for wrongful death, the court held that an insurer, 'has the duty to use reasonable care not to issue a life insurance policy . . . in favor of a beneficiary who has no interest in the continuation of the life of the insured.' A breach of this duty "is the proximate cause of the death of the insured if the verifier of facts finds that this result was reasonably foreseeable." In another famous court case of *Life Insurance Company of Georgia* v. *Lopez*, the insured claimed that the insurer's negligence had endangered his life and caused him injury. The total annual family income was about $ 9,000, but between 1974 and 1977 the insured's wife obtained policies on his life totaling $ 130,000, plus double indemnity for accidental death; the annual premiums were $ 7,464.38. The insured did not know of the life insurance policy purchases. He was tricked into signing the forms, believing his wife was buying health insurance. In 1977, he heard "his wife and her brother plotting to kill him." He called the insurance agent and told him, but no inquiry was made by the insurer. A few months later his wife and her brother tried to drown him, but he was rescued by a passing sheriff. The insured alleged that the insurer should have discovered the disproportionate life insurance coverage on him in relation to the family finances and the company should have investigated the murder conspiracy after getting the actual notice from the insured. The court held that when the insurer has an actual notice of the beneficiary's murderous intent the insurer would be liable if the beneficiary tries to murder the insured to collect the policy proceeds. Notice of the beneficiary's intentions "should have triggered an investigation which would quickly have discovered the disparity between the insured's economic worth and the beneficiary's relative interest in the insured dead or alive, the insured's lack of consent . . . and the financial incongruity of paying premiums regularly for very long period.[6]

Box 4.2

In a much older court judgment, *Liberty National Life Insurance Company v. Weldon case*, there were policies totaling $6,500 on the life of a child who was about two-and-a-half-years-old at the time of her death. The applicant and beneficiary on the policies was the child's aunt-in-law. She murdered the child. A legal suit against the insurer for wrongful death was brought by the child's father, whose argument was that the applicant-beneficiary had no insurable interest in the child's life that the insurers knew or should have discovered the malafides, and their negligence was a proximate cause of the murder of the child to collect the insurance proceeds. Judgment for the father for $75,000 was affirmed by the court. The court pronounced that the amount of recovery under the wrongful death statute was intended to serve as punishment and deterrence for the insurers. The insurers argued that the beneficiary is presumed to know the law, that the policies were illegal and void, due to no insurable interest; hence, those policies could not have been an inducement to kill. However, the court held that, since the beneficiary was convicted of the murder of the child, she must have thought the policies were valid and collectible, and this was the motive for murder. The "jury was well justified in finding that none of" the insurers made a reasonable effort, before issuing the policies, to ascertain whether the beneficiary had an insurable interest in the child's life. The court ruled that a life insurer has a duty to use reasonable care not to issue a life insurance policy in favor of a beneficiary who has no insurable interest in the insured. Murder of the child was reasonably foreseeable, and the insurers created a situation which "afford[ed] temptation to a recognizable percentage of humanity to commit murder." When an insurer fails to fulfill his duty to use reasonable care to avoid issuing a policy where the beneficiary has no interest in the continuation of the life of the insured, that breach of duty will be deemed the proximate cause of the death of the insured if that result was reasonably foreseeable.[7]

Therefore, most courts assume that murder of the insured is a foreseeable event if the beneficiary has no insurable interest in the insured's life. The Indian insurance law requires that the applicant/owner of a life insurance policy, when that applicant himself is not the insured, must have an interest in the continuation of the insured's life (insurable interest). Certain close family relationships, such as spouse, parent, child, or pecuniary interest relationships such as business-key-person or debtor-creditor are presumed to create an insurable interest as discussed ibid. Even if a blood/family relationship exits insurable interest is limited to the amount of financial loss expected on the death of the insured and any over-insurance would defy the principle of insurable interest.

Box 4.3

"Policies in violation of the insurable interest rule are not dangerous because they are illegal; they are illegal because they are dangerous. Practically all courts recognize that "an insured is placed in a position of extreme danger where a policy of insurance is issued on his life in favor of a beneficiary who has no insurable interest."[8]

Suicide

Some insured life insurance policy-holders, if they feel that their family will be better off with the insurance benefit, may be tempted to see suicide as a gainful option. Insurance companies have exclusion clauses[9] in the policy which stipulate that insurance money will not be paid to the beneficiary in case of suicide within a given period of taking the policy. In India most companies have a suicide clause of one year. However, the one year time period in some countries has been found insufficient and has been extended to two years. The exclusion clause is a deterrent only in a limited way as suicide can be difficult to prove and can be made to appear as an accident.[10]

In past few years the issue has gathered concern in Japan as there has been a rise in suicide cases where the person who committed suicide was insured for significantly high sums. Japanese insurance companies have increased their exclusion clause of suicide to a three year period. Here it must be noted that there are cases where insureds carefully plot their own murder making it difficult for the insurance company to prove that the insured committed suicide.

Box 4.4

The following excerpts from an article by *J. Sean Curtin* (Fellow, GLOCOM) and *Earl H. Kinmonth* (Professor, Taisho University) mentions the steps taken by life insurance companies in Japan to counter the increasing number of insurance claim oriented suicide cases. "Although historically Japan has been in the middle of the pack in terms of the reported suicide rates of advanced, industrialized societies, in the last few years the suicide rate for upper middle aged men has gone up significantly. This increase has even had a measurable impact on the overall life expectancy of males. Many such suicides are for the purpose of generating a life insurance payment that will cover the debts of the individual.

'. . . The media has given a fair amount of coverage to the measures life insurance companies have taken to discourage heavily indebted people from taking out policies and then committing suicide so that their families receive large sums of money. Until a few years ago, the majority of life insurance firms had a one-year exemption period for benefit payments in cases where policyholders commit suicide. However, the massive growth in the number of financially-related suicides, foreed most life insurers to extend the exemption period from one-year to two or three-years. Life insurance companies took this measure because they noticed a steep jump in suicide cases immediately after the former one-year suicide nonpayment period expired.' . . . As you observe, because of the prevalence of suicides for the purpose of generating a life insurance payment, Japanese life insurance companies belatedly imposed a two-year minimum coverage period before they would pay out on death by suicide. However, this has now led to a notable spike in deaths in the 25th month of coverage. . . .

'The two to three-year period was believed to discourage indebted people who were contemplating suicide from taking out a life insurance policy. Most Japanese life insurance firms now have a minimum two-year non-payment exemption for suicide. If the recent reports of a spike in suicides just after the two-year suicide exemption period ends are true, then presumably a three-year non-payment threshold will become the norm.'

'Because policies typically pay more for death by accident or violence at the hands of a third party, some people have taken to advertising on the internet for someone who will turn what would otherwise be a suicide into a murder or "accident". A recent *Nihon Keizai Shimbun* article "Netto de satsujin irai" [Turning to the Internet for a Killer] (25 December 2003, p. 17) that dealt with several documented cases of people advertising on the internet for someone who would kill the advertiser for a fee.

Source : Social Trends #64: January 5, 2004, Suicide in Japan: Part Two—The Impact of the Suicide Rate on Life Insurance Policies).

Lapse

Lapse takes place when the applicant is over-insured and later realizes that he cannot afford the insurance premium for the policy and discontinues the policy. The risk of lapse though seems insignificant compared to the above two risks mentioned in the foregoing discussion, it is still a major risk from life insurance company's perspective as an early discontinuation of policies means that the expenses involved in sourcing the application, the agent's commission, the medical testing and the processing and underwriting costs which account for most of the premium in the first few years of the policy cannot be recouped.

Box 4.5

Poor Financial Underwriting and its impact on Mortality

"The Manulife Reinsurance Large Amount Mortality Study published in 1999 provides a breakdown of experience among US reinsurers for the period 1987-96. Experience is analyzed by sum assured and one can see that over the 1988-91 years period, the category of 'sum assured>$5 million' had the worst mortality experience. In fact, the loss ratio was 235% of that of the $3-5 million band. One would expect a better loss ratio with increased sums assured as lives become more affluent and enjoy better standard of living. However, during this period the level of financial underwriting was poor. When this issue was focused upon, the situation improved, and the loss ratio of >$5 million band shrank to 95% of that for the $ 3-5 million category for the period between years 1992-96."[11]

INDIVIDUAL FINANCIAL UNDERWRITING GUIDELINES

Financial underwriting plays an important role in giving only the appropriate amount of insurance to applicants. This protects the life insurance companies from excessive claims. As discussed in previous chapters any deviation from the expected mortality that is not quantified by the underwriters and charged a higher premium, adversely affects the insurance company's financial viability. To ensure that the insurance amount is not large enough to induce murder, suicide or lapse, the insurance companies have evolved guidelines which require substantial documentation and an assessment of the financial, social and behavioral standing of the applicant before granting him life insurance. Financial guidelines require that persons applying for high sums of insurance have to submit relevant documents to prove the need for the applied insurance amount. The guidelines are mentioned below.

Amount of Insurance Cover Allowed

The various criteria that underwriters take into consideration in allowing the sum assured for individuals are given in subsequent paragraphs.

Individuals with Earned Income: The guidelines for maximum insurance cover allowed for individuals for earned income is given below.

Age	*Amount allowed as insurance cover*
18 to 30	22 to 25 times of gross annual income
30 to 40	15 to 17 times of gross annual income
40 to 50	10 to 12 times of gross annual income
50 to 60	5 to 7 times of gross annual income

(Earned income means compensation from participation in a business, including wages, income from salary, tips, commissions and bonuses.)

Individuals with Unearned Income: An individual's income derived from sources other than employment, such as interest and dividends from investments, or income from rental property is defined as unearned income. For such individuals maximum 5 to 10 times of unearned income is allowed for life insurance coverage.

For avoiding unreasonable loss to life insurance companies limiting the sum assured is not sufficient. Limiting the sum assured does not work across all insurance products as effectively. It is so because as different products of insurance have different premium rates. Therefore, to ensure affordability of premium as also to protect the company against early lapse of policies the following guidelines are followed with regard to premium.

Income range of applicant	*Percentage of income allowed as premium*
Income below 2 lacs	10%
Income between 2 to 5 lacs	20%
Income above 5 lacs	30%

Documentation Required for Financial Underwriting

Financial underwriting is solely based on the income of the applicant. Income is one of the questions in the application form. Just as medical tests are called for in high amounts of insurance for medical underwriting a number of financial documents are required to support the income mentioned in the application form (for purpose of financial underwriting for larger sums of life insurance cover). The standard requirement of documents for financial underwriting in most of the life insurance companies are as follows:

- *Sum Assured below Rs. 10 lacs:* No need of financial documents
- *Between Rs. 10 to Rs. 20 lacs*: Financial forms or questionnaires and in some cases income tax returns.
- *Above Rs. 20 lacs*: Income Tax returns for past 3 years/ Profit-loss statement and balance sheets, duly certified by a registered Chartered Accountant.

Undisclosed Income

In India it is commonly seen that some applicants have undisclosed income which does not show on the income tax returns or balance sheets. Many applicants state a higher income in the application form but their income tax returns do not reflect the same amount of income. This happens usually in case of business men/families. In such cases some unconventional income proofs need to be used. Car ownership, credit card limit, property ownership, etc. can provide reasonable estimate of an applicant's income. Some of these substitute (surrogate) income proofs and their use are discussed below.

The overall limit of granting life insurance cover based on the surrogate documents is limited to around Rs. 20-25 lacs as the income established from these documents is at best an estimate. There are certain guidelines* followed by life insurance companies which specify the following details:

(1) Exact documents required?
(2) How to establish the income of the applicant from the surrogate documents?
(3) What multiple to use for calculating the sum assured.

Bank Statements

- *Documents required*: Last 6 months bank statement of the applicants accounts.
- *Income*: Income taken as the average of monthly account balance for last six months × 12.
- *Maximum Sum Assured that can be given*: Income × 10 times limited to a maximum of Rs 25 lacs.

Rent from House Property

- *Income*: Income taken as equivalent to the monthly rent × 12.
- *Documents Required*: Legal rent papers/lease deed.
- *Maximum Sum Assured that can be given*: Income × 10 times limited to a maximum of Rs. 25 lacs.

Home Loans taken from a Scheduled Bank

- *Documents Required*: Repayment schedule and loan sanction letter from the bank. Loan should have been taken at least one year before and there should be no default on the payment of installments.
- *Income*: Income is taken as equal to the monthly installment (EMI) × 12 × 3.
- *Maximum Sum Assured that can be given*: Income x 10 times limited to a maximum of Rs. 25 lacs.

* The guidelines mentioned here are indicative. Different life insurance companies have their own variations of the same.

Fixed Deposits or Investments

- *Documents Required*: Investment papers.
- *Income*: Income is taken equivalent to annual Interest of fixed deposits, RBI bonds, government bonds.
- *Maximum Sum Assured that can be given*: Income × 10 times limited to a maximum of Rs. 25 lacs.

Vehicle Ownership

- *Documents Required*: Car registration and insurance papers.
- *Income*: Income is taken equivalent to insurance value of the car assumed.
- *Maximum Sum Assured that can be given*: Income × 10 times limited to a maximum of Rs. 25 lacs.

Credit Card Ownership

- *Documents Required*: Credit Card photocopy and latest credit card statement.
- *Income*: Income is taken as Rs. 2.5 lacs for Silver card, Rs. 3.5 lacs for a Gold card and Rs. 4.5 lacs for a Platinum card.
- *Maximum Sum Assured that can be given*: Income × 10 times limited to a maximum of Rs. 25 lacs.

Life Insurance Companies don't allow the substitute/ surrogate proofs for insurance above Rs. 25 lacs. The Income Tax Return or balance sheets showing adequate income is a must for life insurance coverage above this amount.

BUSINESS INSURANCE UNDERWRITING GUIDELINES

Human capital (the value that human beings bring to the business) is an important component in a business. It is as important for the success of the company as is the capital represented by machinery, equipment and tangible assets. A company's success depends on the quality and motivation of its employees especially in present day service sector economy.

Key persons in a business be they employees, business owners or partners control and manage the affairs of the organization in an experienced and efficient way to achieve the objectives and targets of the companies. Loss of these persons and the associated financial risk due to their death therefore, can have serious consequences for the company. Their loss may even threaten the very existence of the company, particularly, small and medium-sized enterprises and family businesses. This risk is considerably greater to a company's existence than, say, damage to company's premises, machinery or even business interruption following a disaster. Consequently, appropriate risk coverage measures in the area of human capital are as important, if not more, as in the area of other assets.[12]

The financial risk in these cases is related to the key employee or partner's contribution to the *business results, credit availability and goodwill.* In case of such key persons death the company or firm may face a decline in sales and profits. Such losses are grave and create the problem of looking for a replacement. In case of a partnership firm, death of a partner apart from creating business impediments, can create issues of inheritance of partners' share by heirs and also the associated transitional troubles. Here, a partnership policy can help to keep the continuity of the business, make compensatory payments to buy the share of the deceased from his heirs.

A human capital policy should be purchased in the company's interest by the company itself. The company should, therefore, be the policyholder, the beneficiary as well as the payer of the premiums. Thus the company being the applicant is required to submit financial documents to support the insurance sum applied for. The insured persons can be a key employee or director of a corporation/private or public limited company or all partners of a partnership firm. In case of a director of a private limited company he may be partial owner with shareholding. But his shareholding should not be a majority shareholding as then the insurance will in effect become a personal (individual) insurance and will be underwritten as per the insurance guidelines for individual insurance. The partner or key employee being the prospective 'insured' has to undergo medical tests and answer all questions pertaining to medical and non-medical issues given in the life insurance application form.

Key Person Insurance Underwriting

Key person insurance is used to cover the business or company on demise of that key person. Insurance can reimburse the company for the economic losses it will suffer because of the loss of a profit-maker. The company is the applicant/proposer for the insurance, pays the premiums and is the owner of the policy. The key person is the life insured.

The purpose of key person insurance underwriting is to financially evaluate the appropriate sum for insurance cover for a key person. In financial underwriting the two main factors are firstly, the key person's contribution to the business result and seocndly, the amount of the sum insured.

Factors Considered for Underwriting of Key Persons

Is the Insured a Key-person?

A key-person is the person who contributes significantly to the business profits. A person cannot be insured if he or she does not contribute significantly to the business profits. The principle of insurable interest, viz. the worth of the key person for the business has to be established to avoid any malpractice or potential fraud. Therefore, the relevant questions for the underwriter to ask for are:

- Is the person in question really a key person?
- What is his position in the company?
- What are his activities and responsibilities?
- What is his professional background, educational qualifications and experience?
- What is his contribution to business profits?

This is gathered by information such as Curriculum Vitae of key person and his job profile and designation in the company. A director who is applied for as key man should not hold more than 50% ownership in a Joint Stock company. Together with family members, he should not have more than

70% of the stock in that company. In some cases underwriters allow key man insurance on directors with more than 50% shareholding. However, in such cases the underwriters recognize the fact that the person is actually taking individual cover. Accordingly, they consider the individual income capacity of such key man and include all the individual life insurance covers the person has while assessing the cover that can be allowed and underwrite the case as if it were an individual policy.

The common practice in life insurance industry is to allow key man insurance for a partner if the partnership firm qualifies the following criteria: (a) The annual turn over is at least Rupees 3 crore per annum; and (b) the Key Person is a working partner and not a sleeping partner.[13] The Key Person insurance to employees of a partnership firm follows the same pattern as followed for a private limited company. Key Person Insurance is not available to proprietors of sole proprietorship firms but can be given to employees of sole proprietorship firms.

Does the insurance cover requested for bear an appropriate relation to income/corporate profit and does the company have sufficient financial resources to continue paying the premiums in the future as well?

The insurance amount which can be allowed can be calculated by the annual salary of the key-person, the profits of the company or any loan taken by the company from a bank or registered creditor. The following are three comon ways to evaluate the maximum allowed cover for a key person:

1. Multiple of Salary Approach

In cases where the amount of salary is used for computing the permissible life insurance cover of a key person a general rule is to allow maximum cover equivalent to ten times the annual salary. It is a known fact that within the period of insurance annual salary can vary with increasing specialization or for other reasons as well. But the above mentioned calculations is generally accepted based on current salary. In order to define the annual salary comprehensively and make an objective assessment, it is necessary to know the complete remuneration package. Senior executive staff often receive various fringe benefits (performance-related bonuses, club membership, car expenses, etc.) which also have to be granted to a potential replacement. The annual salary is, therefore, to be understood as a recognized benchmark for corresponding replacement cost.

2. Multiple of the Company Profit Approach

The concerned company's profits are another possible benchmark. In this method a distinction is made between—net profits (which for tax reasons are often kept artificially low), and—gross profits (where proof of fixed costs are to be shown). It is recommended that the maximum sum insured should not exceed three times the annual gross profit averaged out over the last 3 years.

Finally, regarding this approach, it should be remembered that company's losses require special attention. Also newly established companies should be looked at with particular care. In such cases financial ratios such as Current Ratio (current assets/current liabilities) an indicator of debt paying ability of the business, Acid-Test Ratio (cash assets/current liabilities) which assesses how well a company can cover its short-term obligations are analyzed by the underwriters. For new companies an assessment of the above financial ratios is done along with a study of the business plan. It is to be noted that each case is unique in the financial underwriting of the key person. Basically, the aim of underwriting should be to ascertain the consequential cost of the early loss of a key person which include the following:

- estimated loss of profits.
- costs of searching for a replacement.

As a thumb rule the underwriter makes an average of 3 years net profit of the concerned company and multiplies it by 5 to arrive at the sum assured that can be given under a key person life insurance policy. This amount is distributed among the total number of key persons who have applied for insurance. An alternative to this method is to multiply the annual salary of the key person by 10 to arrive at the maximum insurance that can be given. If the company is making major losses usually the underwriters do not allow the company to take a key person policy because if the company is in a loss there can be a risk of fraud. An insurance policy is meant to compensate loss from death of a key person. In case of a loss making company, the company may profit from the insurance benefit it receives from the policy if the key man dies, which is against the principle of insurable interest.

Box 4.6

How much key-man cover should be given?

Example—using multiple of profit approach

3 key persons of a company apply for insurance

Company's net profit is Rs. 25 lacs

25 × 5 = Rs. 1.25 crore

Maximum key person insurance coverage that can be given to each key person is 1.25/3 = Rs. 41 lacs each.

Example—using annual salary approach

Two key persons apply for insurance

Each has an annual salary of Rs. 10 lacs each

The maximum key person insurance cover that can be given is Rs. 1 crore to each.

3. Loan Amount-related Approach

In this approach of financial underwriting the sum insured is linked to the size of the loan or mortgage. The term period of the cover should be arranged to coincide with the term period of the loan.

DOCUMENTS REQUIRED FOR KEY PERSON INSURANCE

The following documents are required for financial underwriting on a key-person life insurance application:

1. Profit and Loss Account of the Company for past 3 years. (duly audited by a registered chartered accountant)

2. Key Person Questionnaire. (duly filled)
3. Articles of Association and memorandum of association in a Private Ltd. Company. Deed of partnership in a partnership concern.
4. Board resolution to buy Key Person Insurance policy. Deed of variation in the case of partnership concern for decision to take a key person policy.
5. Income Tax Returns relating to the Key Person for the past 3 Years.

Box 4.7

Sample of a board resolution

CERTIFIED TRUE COPY of an extract from the minutes of the meeting of the Board of Directors of ABC Pvt. Ltd. duly convened at Byavasaya Puram on Date, Month, Year.

IT WAS RESOLVED THAT the Company take KEY PERSON POLICY for Rs. 50 lacs in favour of Mr. Khas Admi to safeguard the Company from probable losses in the event of his demise, from XYZ LIFE INSURANCE COMPANY LTD. The premiums of which will be paid by the Company.

FURTHER RESOLVED THAT Mr. Dhan Sanchalak, Chief Financial Officer of the Company be and is authorized to sign all the papers and documents, including Application Form, *as* required by XYZ Life Insurance Co. Ltd. in this regard.

That a copy of foregoing resolution duly certified to be true copy, be furnished to the XYZ Life Insurance Co. Ltd.

Partnership Insurance

Partnership firms are also concerned about protecting the company from the adversities of death of a profit generating partner. Consequently, for a partnership firm a partnership insurance becomes a necessity because in case of a partner's death a partnership concern may dissolve and a new partnership has to be constituted. The heir of the dead partner may come into the business in some cases. A surviving partner may not want interference in the business from the heir who may be unqualified or inexperienced. In such cases the surviving partner may want to buy the shares of the deceased from the heirs by paying a lump sum money. Insurance policies can be an ideal funding vehicle for this purchase. Partnership insurance allows surviving business partners to purchase an individual partner's share of the business from the insurance proceeds from the deceased's heirs. Accordingly this type of insurance is also called 'buy-sell insurance'. The buy-sell clause is added to the partnership deed (agreement) which specifies that all the monetary death benefits from the insurance policy be used for buying partners shares only. This buy-sell provision is made through a supplementary deed or a deed of variation and is the legal arrangement designed to provide for an orderly transfer of ownership.

Partnership insurance is useful to surviving owners. It provides funds to purchase the business interest held by the heirs. It also assures the surviving owners control of the company, as in such case the heirs must sell the shares to the firm and not to outsiders. The surviving partner or partners are guaranteed full management control by eliminating the possibility that the heirs will assume management positions for which they are not qualified. It also eliminates potential emotional conflicts between the heirs and the surviving business owners—conflicts that could impair the harmonious operation of the company. Such an insurance cover also eliminates pressures on the surviving owners to contribute some parts of the profits to the family of the deceased partner. For the deceased partner it assures that his heirs/family will get a lump sum payment without any hassel to the extent the deceased partner had realistically wished and planned during his life time.

.To determine the amount of insurance that the partners should be given the underwriter must know the value of each partner's interest in the business and the firm's gross and net profits.

Guidelines: Procedures and Processes (Partnership Insurance)

Under partnership insurance the firm is the applicant/ proposer and owner of the policy.

The objective of insurance is to protect the firm against loss of profit on the death of a partner. All the partners in the firm should be insured under a partnership insurance cover. If one partner is uninsurable or if he is over insurable age the same can be explicitly mentioned in the agent's letter.

The sum assured of the policy on the life of a partner should have a reasonable relationship to the expected loss. It should match the amount expected to be paid out on the death of the partner to buy his shares from the heirs. A golden rule that is usually applied is that the sum assured is the value of the share capital of the partner. Another easy calculation to arrive at the maximum insurable sum is five times of average of last three years net profit divided among the partners based on their share percentage.

The financial documents like balance sheets of the firm, the supplementary deed and other relevant questionnaires are required by the insurance companies to assess the insurable amount and other pertinent aspects of the case before issuing the policy.

Box 4.8

Example for calculating maximum sum assured for partnership cover

Net profit of partnership firm Rs. 25 lacs

Allowed Insurance 25 × 5 = Rs. 1.25 crores

Three partners in the firm with 33% share each

Insurance for each partner Rs. 1.25 crores/3= Rs. 41.6 lacs

If one partner is uninsurable then on proof of un-insurability, a sum of Rs. 62.5 lacs can be given to the other two partners.

Box 4.9

Buy-sell (Supplementary Deed) on a stamp Papar

Notwithstanding anything stated in the Partnership Deed Dated ——— and or any other document We, the partners of the ...... ("Firm") hereby agree:

1. *That Life Insurance Policy of Rs .... be purchased on the life of ——————————— (Partner(s) of the Firm) for which premium shall be charged to the Firm;*
2. That on death of any partner, insured pursuant to this Deed of Variation, the proceeds of such Policy shall be utilized by the Firm solely to purchase the share of the deceased partner in the Firm;
3. That in the event of dissolution of the Firm, during the life of the policy, the policy will be surrendered for its then surrender value or assigned to the Life insured as the case may be;

4. That Mr./Mrs./Ms. .... working as .... in the firm is authorized to sign all the papers on behalf of the Firm in connection with the Life Insurance Policies .

Dated at....................this............. day of.............................. 2001.

Signatures of Partners

Partner __________

Partner_______________

Witnesses:

Signature of the Witness:________________________

Name of the Witness: ____________________

Address of the Witness: _________________

Of all the non-medical information presented to the underwriter for key man insurance purposes, the information about the applicant's finances, income and financial reputation is of utmost importance. Statistics show that if a person buys more life insurance than he or she can afford, the company's mortality experience is likely to be adversely affected as they indicate the possibility of speculation and anti-selection.[14] To be able to understand the case clear and better the underwriter must use the agent as an important tool and source of information for financial underwriting purposes. A Cover letter from *the agent* provides the underwriter with a comprehensive source of "up front" information. This means less hassle for the client, faster underwriting and quicker issue of the policy. Cover letters are helpful in all cases and more so for applicant company's requirement for larger amounts of insurance.

The Agent's Letter for personal insurance the letter must highlight the following information: (a) background information of the sale, (b) purpose of the coverage, (c) how the proposed sum was determined, (d) total insurance applied for with the insurance company or other companies if applicable, (e) insurance already in-force, (f) replacement details (i.e. policies in-force which will be discontinued once the new policy is issued), (g) applicant's income and net worth, and (h) full listing of assets and liabilities (duly attested by a Chartered Accountant).

For business insurance coverage the agent's letter should highlight the following: (a) purpose of coverage, (b) how amount was determined, (c) job function and percentage of ownership (if any) in the company, (d) descriptions of and projections pertaining to loan agreements if applicable, (e) projections on new business ventures, and (f) any other information that the agent feels may provide better insight into the case.

Another important source of information that some of the life insurance companies use is the 'Financial questionnaire'. This questionnaire is required for proposed insurance amounts above a certain level. It contains details about (a) the source of income, (b) family members, (c) household income and expenses, and (d) other relevant aspects that can help the underwriter to form a clear picture of the applicant's social and financial status.

Notes and References

1. The person(s) or entity(ies) (e.g. corporation, trust, etc.) named in the policy as the recipient of insurance proceeds upon the death of the insured.
2. *Source*: website-http://www.transamericareinsurance.com/associate_article.asp?Id=22
3. *Source*: website-http://ahtins.com/glossary/fff/f040.htm.
4. *Source*: Life Underwriting Newsletter, Second issue of the Munich Re Life Underwriting Newsletter!
5. An Insurer's Duty to Investigate by John Dwight Ingram, Florida State University, College of Law.
6. *Source*: website-https://www.law.fsu.edu/current_students organizations/businessreview/vol3/ingram.pdf
7. *Source*: website-https://www.law.fsu.edu/current_students/organizations/businessreview/vol3/ingram.pdf
8. Source: website-https://www.law.fsu.edu/current_students/organizations/businessreview/vol3/ingram.pdf
9. Exclusion Clauses are expressly eliminated from the coverage of an insurance contract or policy. Examples of general exclusions are suicide or suicide attempt, acts of war, or foreign travel.
10. Stuart Land, FIA, FASSA, The Actuary India, Oct. 2003.
11. *Source*: Article 'Financial Underwriting' by Stuart Land FIA, FASSA in the October 2003 issue of the Actuary India.
12. Overview of Financial Underwriting by Wayne Macedo, Vice President and Chief Underwriter, International Division Transamerica Reinsurance.
13. A sleeping partner is a partner in a trade, or shop, who lends his name and money, for which he receives a share of the profit, without doing any part of the business.
14. Anti-selection is the tendency of people who have a greater-than-average likelihood of loss to seek insurance coverage to a greater extent than individuals who have an average or less-than-average likelihood of loss. It is also known as adverse selection. and is discussed in greater detail in Chapter 7, New Frontiers.

Chapter 5

Medical Tests

Learning Objectives

The material in this chapter should enable the reader to understand

- Medical tests usually required with a life insurance application.
- Preparation guidelines for clients before a medical test.
- Raised blood sugar, blood pressure, cholesterol and liver enzymes in asymptomatic and apparently healthy clients.

CHAPTER

5

Medical Tests

MEDICAL TESTS

The concept of Uberrima Fides (utmost good faith) is an underlying principle in life insurance contract. In its applied sense, the applicant is obliged to answer all questions in the application form truthfully and accurately. He must also disclose all material facts without holding back any relevant details. Some applicants may try to conceal pertinent information of adverse conditions that an insurance company cannot discover without their co-operation in order to facilitate acceptance of the application. When a deliberate non-disclosure or misrepresentation, of an existing adverse medical or non-medical condition, comes to light through random verification or through investigation at the time of claim the policy is rendered null and void and the claim is not honored. The concept of utmost good faith seeks to control and reduce non disclosures. However, some legal clauses as discussed below exist in the insurance contract which may make it difficult for life insurance companies to avoid claims even in cases of non disclosure, thus serving as protective measures for the insuring public against the sometimes overzealous endeavors of insurance companies to repudiate the claims in cases of non-disclosure and misrepresentation.

(1) Most life insurance policies carry a two-year "incontestable clause" which prevents the life insurance company from calling into question a policy, after the expiry of two years from the date on which it came into effect, on the basis that there was a misrepresentation in the application form or medical report or any document which led to the issue of the policy. Only in cases where the life insurance company can prove that the policy-holder had made a fraudulent misrepresentation on a material fact the policy can be made void after expiry of the contestable period.
(2) Accidental misrepresentation can occur when the applicant is unaware of the severity of his medical condition. Also, questions may not be understood by applicants for example—diabetics who are controlled by diet alone can answer 'No' to a question of having high blood sugar. Unless the policy-holder dies within the incontestable period the insurance company will find it difficult to repudiate the claim.
(3) Possible legal battle between the company and the family of the deceased insured on repudiating a claim has a cost associated with it in terms of investigative and legal fees for the insurance company. The gravity of legal implications in a life insurance policy contract can be discerned clearly by readers from the sample court cases given in Section V of this book.

With a view to avoid unsavory implications as stated above life insurance companies conduct medical examination and medical tests for applicants, particularly so when the applications are for larger sums of life insurance to ensure that the health condition of the applicant is thoroughly investigated at the time of application. The medical-non-medical table in Annexure 3 has a list of tests required based on the age and sum assured of the applicant.

Box 5.1

> As per the "mature book", Guardian Financial Services, ninety per cent of Critical illness claims paid in the past 15 years are from policies more than five years old. These were not routinely checked for non-disclosure of ailments.[1]
>
> Surveys conducted by some life insurance company offices have shown non-disclosure of serious medical conditions of around 15%, and there are many instances of non-disclosure on mail shot applications.[2]

Life insurance companies have a panel of doctors who are deputed to conduct basic medical examinations and a panel of diagnostic centers for blood tests and other specialized tests. The medical examinations may be done by a general medical practitioner or a Medical specialist. For electrocardiographs, insurance companies have cardiologists to conduct tests and report abnormalities, if any. The common medical tests which are required in medical cases are as follows:

- Medical Examination Report (MER).
- Urine Tests (Routine and Microscopic).
- Blood Chemistry-Fasting Blood Sugar, Liver Enzymes tests, kidney function tests, cholesterol levels.
- Blood Tests for HIV and hepatitis.
- Cardiac Tests-Treadmill and Electrocardiograph (ECG).

MEDICAL EXAMINATION REPORT (MER)

MER is the key source of information in a medical case. The underwriters evaluate this information with great care. Doctors doing the MER first establish the identity of the applicant by asking for an Identification proof. MER form consists of two main sections.

Section I: It deals with the medical history and family history of the client. In this section medical questions about each body organ similar to the questions in the proposal form are put to the client by the doctor and client's answers are noted by the examining doctor.

Section II: This section deals with physical details. Record of height, weight, pulse, blood pressure and other medical parameters are entered by the examining doctor in his own hand in this section. Doctors also give their opinion on the health of the client and sign and date the medical examination report. Some medical examination reports also require a urinalysis dipstick test for the levels of sugar or protein in urine. Blood pressure and weight recorded in the MER are two significant pieces of information which the underwriters analyze in deciding the likely mortality risks of the applicant.

Urinalysis

Urinalysis can be a part of the MER or may be a separate test. It may involve a detailed microscopic examination or may be restricted to a dipstick test. The urine is examined chemically and microscopically for the presence of albumin, pus, casts, or red blood cells, which would indicate a diseased condition of the kidneys. Urinalysis also measures the functional capacity of the kidneys, detects infections or other abnormal conditions of the kidneys, and may discover impairments of other vital organs of the body.

Urinalysis can Detect

- kidney problems
- urinary infections
- presence of sugar in the urine (possible diabetes)

Blood Chemistry

Fasting Blood Sugar (FBS)

Fasting Blood sugar is a common test for life insurance applicants. Fasting Blood Sugar can be either a part of the biochemistry test or a stand alone test. This test detects the level of sugar in the blood. The normal range of blood sugar is between 60 to 109 mg./dl. A level above this range indicates diabetes. For life insurance purposes an underwriter categorizes even people with a blood sugar level of 100 as diabetic, especially if it is associated with adverse risk factors such as obesity, smoking or adverse family history. Probability of such persons developing complications associated with diabetes is very high.

Liver Enzymes (Liver Function Tests)

One of the components of bio chemistry blood examination is liver enzymes. The components of this test are AST (also called SGOT), ALT (also called SGPT), GGT and Alkaline Phosphatase.[3] These liver enzymes help all the chemical activities within cells to take place. Injury to cells of the liver releases these enzymes into the blood elevating their level above normal limits. Damage to the liver due to over-consumption of alcohol as well as occurrence of liver diseases, results in increased levels of these enzymes. These enzymes are also found in some other cells of the body apart from the liver such as muscles and heart. Consequently raised levels of these enzymes may not necessarily be due to liver injury or disease in all cases. AST/SGOT, ALT/SGPT are liver and muscle enzymes. They may be elevated from liver problems, hepatitis, excess alcohol ingestion, muscle injury and recent heart attack. GGT is also elevated in liver disease, particularly with obstruction of bile ducts. An elevated level of enzymes indicates disease of the liver. Alkaline phosphatase is an enzyme found primarily in bones and the liver. Enzyme levels are higher for growing children and pregnant women or when damage to bones or liver has occurred. Gallstones also give rise to increased enzyme levels. Low enzyme values are generally not significant.

Bilirubin is a yellow breakdown product of normal heme metabolism. When red blood cells die, the heme in their hemoglobin is converted to bilirubin in the spleen and in the hepatocytes in the liver. The bilirubin is processed by the liver, enters bile and is eventually excreted through feces. Its levels are elevated in certain diseases and it is responsible for the yellow color of bruises and the brown color of feces. Low values of bilirubin are of no concern. An increase in bilirubin results in a condition called jaundice in which the skin and eyes turn yellowish. Jaundice can occur due to liver diseases and gall stones. Some diseases which increase the rate of hemolysis (breakdown of red blood cells) also manifest as jaundice thus an increase in bilirubin is always investigated by the underwriter.

Kidney Function Tests

Kidney functions are reflected by measuring the Blood Urea Nitrogen (BUN), Creatinine and Uric Acid levels in the blood. BUN is a waste substance produced in the liver and excreted by the kidneys. Elevated levels of BUN may mean that the kidneys are not functioning as well as they should. BUN is also affected by high protein diets and/or strenuous exercise which raise its levels. Creatinine is also a waste product of the body. High creatinine values, especially along with high BUN levels, may indicate problems with the kidneys. Uric Acid is normally excreted in urine. Here also high values are indicative of health problems and may be associated with gout, arthritis and kidney problems.

Cholesterol

Cholesterol is a fat-like substance in the blood. High level of cholesterol in blood has been associated with narrowing of arteries due to deposits of fat on the walls of the arteries and thus causing heart disease. The various categories of lipids in blood are High density lipoproteins (HDL), low density lipoproteins (LDL) and very low density lipoproteins (VLDL). Triglycerides is another form in which fat exists in blood.

Total Cholesterol: High cholesterol in the blood is a major risk factor for heart and blood vessel diseases. Cholesterol in itself is not all bad; in fact, our bodies need a certain amount of cholesterol to function properly. As the level of blood cholesterol increases, so does the possibility of plugging the arteries due to cholesterol plaque build-up. This process is called "hardening of the arteries" or atherosclerosis which is a adverse health condition. When the arteries feeding the heart get plugged, a heart attack may occur. If the arteries that go to the brain are affected, then the result is a stroke.

LDL Cholesterol is considered "bad cholesterol" because cholesterol deposits occur in the arteries when LDL levels are high. HDL cholesterol is a 'good cholesterol' as it protects against heart disease by helping remove excess cholesterol deposited in the arteries. High levels of HDL seem to be associated with low incidence of coronary heart disease.

Triglyceride is fat in the blood which, if elevated, has been associated with heart disease. VLDL is another carrier of fat in the blood.

Table 5.1
Normal Values
(Indicative Values for Adult Males)

Test	*Normal Range*
Blood Sugar	<110
BUN	10 - 20 mg/dL
Creatinine	<1.5 mg/dL
Uric Acid	3.5 - 7.5 mg/dl
SGOT (AST)	0 - 42 U/L
SGPT (ALT)	0 - 48 U/L
GGT	0 - 65 U/L
Alk. Phos.	20 - 125 U/L
Bilirubin	0 - 1.3 mg/dl
Total Cholesterol	Less than 225 mg/dL
HDL	35 - 135 mg/dl
Triglycerides	0 - 200 mg/dl
LDL	62 - 130 mg/dl
VLDL	20 - 40 mg/dl

Human Immunodeficiency Virus (HIV) and Hepatitis

Persons applying for large amount of life insurance polices are tested for HIV and Hepatitis. HIV is a virus that steadily weakens the body's defense (immune) system until it can no longer fight off infections such as pneumonia, diarrhea, tumors and other illnesses. All of which can be part of AIDS (Acquired Immunodeficiency Syndrome). With the body unable to fight off infections, most people die within three years of the first appearing signs of AIDS. HIV infections mostly are transmitted through unprotected sexual intercourse with someone who is already infected with HIV. HIV can also be transmitted by infected blood or blood products (as in blood transfusions), by sharing contaminated needles and from an infected woman to her baby before birth, during delivery, or through breast-feeding. HIV is not transmitted through touch, lavatory seats, sharing of sofas or day-to-day contacts.

Hepatitis is inflammation of the liver. Hepatitis can be caused by viruses, bacteria, alcohol, toxic chemicals and certain drugs. Symptoms include jaundice (yellowish skin caused by the buildup of bile pigments in the body), fever, loss of appetite and gastrointestinal upset. There are different variants of Hepatitis. Hepatitis A is not fatal and may be transmitted by drinking or eating contaminated food, by fecal-oral contact, and/or through household contact. Hepatitis A may be mild to severe; symptoms include fever, nausea, and jaundice. Hepatitis B Virus (HBV) can cause severe liver damage and even death. It is typically spread by blood or body fluid contact, such as through hypodermic syringes or sexual intercourse. A type of liver cancer called hepatoma can also follow HBV infection. Hepatitis C virus is also referred to as nonA-nonB hepatitis and is the most common form of blood transfusion-acquired hepatitis. Hepatitis B and C are the dangerous varieties and both can be detected through blood tests.

Cardiac Tests: Electrocardiograph (ECG) and Treadmill

ECG is a diagnostic procedure used to study the structure and motion of the heart. It involves the recording of the electrical activity of the muscles of the heart which allows diagnosis of cardiac abnormalities. Pacing on a treadmill (a regulated moving platform with speed recording device) which raises the heart beat systematically and gradually by increase of speed of walking accompanied with the recording of electrical impulses of heart on an ECG machine is called the stress ECG or the 'treadmill test'.

PREPARING FOR A MEDICAL TEST

Apart from underlying disease conditions many other factors also affect medical test results. These include physiological factors, patient preparation, specimen collection and its transport. Also the precision and accuracy of the test method and factors like lipaemia, *in vitro* haemolysis may interfere with test results. Medications taken by the applicant may also affect medical test results. Incorrect data entry, calculation mistakes by laboratory staff, improper data transfer and the method used to report the results (electronic, paper or telephone) may also result in incorrect result of the test.[4] To ensure that the medical test result does not get skewed due to unprepared-ness or undue anxiety of the applicant the following do's and don't's should be followed when going for life insurance medical test.

Do's

1. Completely fast (no eating) for five hours prior to the examination (no eating) and drink only water.
2. Schedule the medical examination in the early morning, if possible. You may be more relaxed and blood pressure readings are generally at their lowest.
3. Make a list of major illnesses, surgery, or injuries including the record of dates, doctors, hospitals, addresses, and treatment to the extent known. Disclose all such details, as omissions may adversely impact insurability and future claims.
4. If currently taking medications, have the name and dosage available.
5. Have your driving license or other identification proof available for identification.
6. Give the urine specimen before the blood pressure readings as it may lower the reading.
7. Get a good night's sleep prior to the medical examination and be relaxed.

Don'ts

1. *Caffeine*—Do not take coffee or colas before the medical examination as it may adversely affect blood pressure readings.
2. *Cholesterol*—Readings are elevated by red meat, cheese, eggs and saturated fats. Watch your diet for 24 hours before the medical examination.

3. *Exercise*—Sometimes alters urine chemistry. Take it easy for few days prior to the medical examination.
4. *Nicotine*—elevates blood pressure by constricting artery walls. If you use nicotine, in any form, preferably avoid for 24 hours to 48 prior to the medical examination.
5. *Stimulants*—Do not use stimulants such as alcohol and avoid chocolate for at least 24 hours before medical examination. Stimulants are potential causes for temporary elevated blood pressure readings.
6. *Salt*—Have low salt for 3-4 days before the medical examination. Non-consumption of salt may lower the blood pressure reading.

ADVERSE MEDICAL TEST IN ASYMPTOMATIC INDIVIDUALS

When a client is put through medical tests for life insurance and the result is abnormal there can be four reasons:

(1) The client was not aware of the medical problem—Asymptomatic Individuals
(2) There has been an error in the medical test.
(3) The client has not disclosed the fact in the application form.
(4) The client has disclosed the fact and may be willing to pay the extra premium which the company would impose. (This is discussed in detail in Chapter 6)

When the client is apparently healthy and asymptomatic, the medical test results if adverse often come as a surprise to the life insurance agents and their clients. As enumerated in the first point above, it is not uncommon for people with no signs or symptoms of disease to have abnormal medical test result when undergoing a medical test for life insurance. These people may have been suffering from a disease without any overt signs and symptoms which is brought to light at the time of the medical test. Other reasons for abnormal tests results as explained earlier are either the errors in tests or deliberate non disclosure in the application form. Therefore, to take a decision and appropriately rate the applicant, underwriters usually ask for repeat tests if the medical test is abnormal in cases where applicants have not disclosed any health problems. Underwriters also look at the totality of the case. If an applicant is overweight, has a diabetic father and he also smokes there is a very high possibility of his high blood sugar report being accurate as compared to another client who is thin and does not smoke. Medical tests which may give adverse results in asymptomatic individuals are discussed in succeeding paragraphs with a brief outline of the underwriting course of action.

Raised Blood Sugar

It has been documented world over that many people are first diagnosed as diabetics when raised blood sugar is found in their blood at the time of the life insurance medical examination. This is because diabetes is a silent disease. Diabetics may not suffer from any distinctive symptoms in initial stages of the disease. The only way it can be detected is through a fasting blood sugar test. The underwriter usually requests a repeat test to verify the high blood sugar detected if the applicant has no other risk factors such as obesity, family history of diabetes etc. The decision is taken only if the repeat test also shows high blood sugar. If the blood sugar level in the repeat test is very high (more than 150 mg/dl) the case may be postponed for three months until the individual takes treatment. If the blood sugar is below 150 mg/dl the underwriter may decide to rate up the case as per the manual rating for a diabetic. Indicative rating for diabetics is discussed in the next chapter.

Raised Blood Pressure (BP)

Another condition that is commonly detected during a life insurance medical examination is high blood pressure. It is a less common first diagnosis than diabetes as many people with high BP have symptoms which prompt them to see a doctor and so they are aware of their condition.

Most underwriters do not raise the premium only on the basis of high blood pressure reported in the Medical Examination Report. Just as they do for diabetic cases, underwriters look for totality of risk factors to validate the blood pressure recorded by the examining doctor before taking a decision. An overweight applicant who is also a smoker has a higher possibility of having high blood pressure than someone who has normal weight and is a non smoker. The underwriter would investigate the later case further and may call for a re-test to ensure that there has been no error in the recording of blood pressure. Factors which erroneously cause moderately high blood pressure recordings are the following:

- Eating a heavy meal immediately before the test
- Drinking coffee immediately before the test
- Smoking before the test
- Alcohol drinking
- Emotional stress
- Strenuous physical exercise
- Anxiety/tension of visiting a doctor

To rule out the above reasons for inaccurate blood pressure recording the underwriter requests for repeat blood pressure recording (typically, three recordings at five minute intervals) especially when the applicant does not have any predisposing risk factors for high blood pressure.

The premium ratings depend on the level of the blood pressure recorded. The rating for applicants with high blood pressure is given in the next chapter. However, as individuals not on treatment have a higher risk of complications, the underwriter may rate up the case more when the applicant has been diagnosed for the first time during the life insurance medical examinations. If the blood pressure reading is very high for example BP >160/100 the case gets postponed till he takes treatment and the blood pressure is under control.

Cholesterol Level

High cholesterol level is another problem which clients may not be aware of and it comes as a surprise to them. High cholesterol levels are related to other disease conditions such as diabetes, high blood pressure, etc. If a client smokes, has family history of diabetes, has high blood pressure or is obese (overweight), he may very likely be detected to have high blood sugar (diabetes), high blood pressure or increased cholesterol level during medical examination.

So when the agent prepares to send the client for the insurance medical test he should review the following factors:

- Smoking
- Family History of Diabetes
- High blood pressure
- Overweight/Obesity

If the applicant discloses these factors while completing the application form he must be informed of the possibility of high cholesterol levels detected in the medical tests. In such cases the DO's and DON'T's should be followed so that the test results are not exacerbated.

Elevated Liver Enzymes

Liver enzymes blood tests are required by life insurance companies to assess the function of liver. Liver is an important organ in the body and plays a critical role in utilizing the consumed food for energy. Liver produces various important ingredients for physical well-being and removes toxins from the body. Liver enzymes are also found in skeletal or cardiac muscles and bones.

Liver enzymes are raised due to following factors:

- Excessive Alcohol intake
- Cirrhosis of liver due to alcohol or liver infection
- Liver diseases (Different type of Hepatitis A, B etc.)
- Diabetes
- High BP
- Cholesterol increase
- Overweight/obesity
- Kidney stones
- Gall bladder stone
- Heart disease

Liver enzymes can also be elevated due to the consumption of antibiotics, painkillers, oral hormone replacement, exposure to toxic chemicals, insecticides and bone diseases or fracture. Therefore, the evaluation and diagnosis of the reason for increased liver enzymes is quite complicated. An underwriter is not concerned about the diagnosis of a disease; he rates up a case based on the level of the enzyme mentioned in the medical test results. So in case of elevated liver enzymes underwriters charge extra premium depending on how much the liver enzymes are elevated from the normal level. Usually a repeat test is requested by an underwriter before rating up such a case.

In this chapter many instances of adverse test results in asymptomatic applicants and its implications from the underwriting point of view have been discussed. It is important to note that underwriters only take a prognostic view of the applicant's health based on the medical reports. Underwriting decisions are not an indication of current clinical health status nor do they provide any medical advice or treatment. Thus, if an abnormality is detected in the insurance medical tests, the applicant should get a recheck done on his own and consult his personal doctor to understand his health condition and take appropriate treatment. In case the applicant finds out that his test result are normal and his personal doctor certifies that there is no medical problem then the case should be properly presented to the underwriting department for a second assessment. A letter from the applicant with attached medical reports may be required for such assessment. Usually the underwriter will request another recheck from the medical centre on their panel before changing the earlier decision on the case. An agent's knowledge on these issues and anticipation of such possibilities helps in establishing a professional image of the life insurance company officials and their company before the insuring public.

Notes and References

1. *Source*: Navigating the critical illness minefield by Jennifer Hill, *The Scotsman*, Sat. 11 Feb. 2006.
2. *Source*: "Underwriting—A Dying Art? By T.S. Leigh, F.I.A., F.C.I.I." *Journal of Institute of Actuaries*, UK.

3. Alanine aminotranferease (ALT) and aspartate aminotransferase (AST) are enzymes located in liver cells that leak out into the general circulation when liver cells are injured. These two enzymes are also known as the serum glutamic-pyruvic transaminase (SGPT) and the serum glutaic-oxaloacetic transaminase (SGOT) respectively.
4. *Source*: Website: http://www.rcpamanual.edu.au/sections/single article.asp?s=70.

Chapter 6

Medical Underwriting

The material in this chapter should enable the reader to understand

- Selection and classification of medical risks through numerical rating system
- Extra Mortality Ratings of common medical ailments
- Reconsideration of rating or decision by the underwriter
- Medical Conditions which lead to rejection-decline or postponement of case

CHAPTER

6

Medical Underwriting

MEDICAL UNDERWRITING, THE CONCEPTS AND PROCESS

Medical Underwriting is the process of selecting risks for life insurance and classifying the applicants according to their degrees of mortality discernable from their health conditions. This is with a view to assess the premium that has to be appropriately charged. In previous chapters we have seen that the cases of occupational, avocational and residential risks are commonly rated using the flat-extra method and the financial risks of a case are evaluated based on income and the sum of insurance applied for. In cases of medical underwriting, both, the nature of extra risk from medical factors and the type of policy are assessed. Unlike occupational, residential and other non-medical risks which are consistent in nature throughout the policy term and are rated up using the flat extra method, medical risks continue to increase with the increase in age. For medical underwriting credit debit system and numerical rating systems are used to classify and rate these risks.

Credit-Debit System

Credit-debit system is the basic tenet of mortality risk assessment. Oscar Rogers and Arthur Hunter mathematically formalized this system for risk selection in early 1900s. They viewed more than 90% of the insurance-buying population group as non-impaired or "standard" lives. This group of standard lives was assigned a value of 100%. Other individuals identified as impaired or non-standard required additional 'debits' to compensate for the expected excess mortality results that they would generate in the insurance pool.[1]

Numerical Rating System

Numerical rating system was devised in USA and was a subject of animated debate in actuarial literature of the 1960s. Under this system, credits are given for favorable factors like good family history or a proportionate body height and weight. Debits are given for unfavorable factors, such as high blood pressure or diabetes. The total accumulation of credit and debit represents a client's percentage of extra mortality, usually taken to the nearest 25%. Thus imposition a 100% extra mortality rating would mean that the applicant, over the duration of the policy, is likely to experience double the mortality risk than a person accepted on standard terms. Comprehensive and detailed indicative extra mortality rates (EMRs) for almost all medical conditions are contained in underwriting manuals.

Numerical ratings are derived from these manuals. Most of the life insurance companies allow standard rates for up to 30% or 50% extra mortality, and even higher extra mortality assessments may be disregarded for those aged under 30 years to avoid relatively small, additional premiums. A combination of flat extra premium plus a percentage extra mortality rating is also a common method of underwriting decision.

The numerical rating method and the EMRs for adverse medical conditions can be used to effectively rate most of the medical impairments. However, for serious impairments, which are independent of age, and remain consistent throughout the life of insured, the underwriters normally impose a flat extra premium. Medical conditions such as cancer fall under this category. Also a combination of impairments, such as diabetes with hypertension, may merit more than an add up of the two impairment ratings. For this a mere clerical reference to manual may not suffice. In such cases the overall EMR must be arrived at with due thought, care and application of medical knowledge, intuition and good judgment.[2]

Extra mortality rates as discussed earlier are imposed in groups of twenty five and are also referred to as risk classes as seen in the Table 6.1.

TABLE 6.1

Classes	*Extra Mortality Rate (EMR)*	*Classes*	*Extra Mortality Rate (EMR)*
1*	0	8	+175
2	+25	9	+200
3	+50	10	+225
4	+75	11	+250
5	+100	12	+300
6	+125	13	+350
7	+150	14	+400

*Class 1 indicates standard rates.

The extra mortality factor imposed on a substandard risk in the process of risk classification is not exact. This means that the risk of an individual insured in each risk class, though consistent to a large extent, is not accurately precise. There is also some degree of variation between risks of each individual in the same group because of small rounding off for all individual risks in each group, known as subsidization. The goal of an insurance company is to reduce subsidization by placing individuals in the risk class closest to their actual extra mortality index. Eliminating the subsidization is not practical as it would mean having a large number or narrowly defined risk classes. It will imply that very few people would be available in each class which will not allow the 'law of large numbers' to operate effectively. The law of large numbers is a critical principle in insurance and it is through the operation of law of large numbers that risk transference becomes commercially feasible.[3]

Translating Extra Mortality into Actual Premium Increase

Translating extra mortality into actual premium increase is dependant on the age of the insured and the plan of insurance applied for. For term plans, 50% extra mortality is equivalent to extra premium of 50% of the standard because the premium of term plan is made up mostly of the mortality component. For plans like whole life or endowment[4] where the premium has significant investment component the extra mortality is applied only on the mortality portion of the premium rate which increases with the increase in age. Premiums of all insurance plans have component of mortality. This component is different in different plans. Shown below is a illustrative table of the premium components in different plans.

Box 6.2

Plan	*Mortality premium*	*Expenses portion*	*Investment*
Whole Life	25 to 40%	20%	40%
Term	Almost 100%	Very little	None
Endowment	10 to 25%	20%	60%

Given above is a broad range of mortality component for whole life and endowment plans. In the table above the age of the applicant and the duration of the policy determine the exact mortality component. Higher the age and longer the policy duration of the whole life plan or endowment plan, the higher the level of extra premium. To assist underwriters to derive the final extra premium based on EMR for different ages and plans, the insurance companies have software programs which calculate the extra premium according to age of the applicant, the type of product, the duration of the policy and the EMR decided by the underwriter. For example, a 50% extra mortality may be equivalent to 15% increase in premium for a whole life and only a 5% increase for an endowment plan for a certain age.[5] In the table given below the range of increases in premium

TABLE 6.3

Age	*Plan*	*Class 2* *EMR + 25*	*3* *50*	*4* *75*	*5* *100*	*6* *125*
21-30	Term	25	50	75	100	125
	Whole Life	6.25%-8.75%	12.5%-17.5%	18.75%-26.25%	25%-35%	31.25%-43.75%
	Endowment	2.5%-3.75%	5% -7.5%	7.5%-11.25%	10%-15%	12.5%-18.75%
31-35	Term	25	50	75	100	125
	Whole Life	7.5%-10%	15%-20%	22.5%-30%	30% -40%	37.5%-50%
	Endowment	2.5%-3.75%	5%-7.5%	7.5%-11.25%	10%-15%	12.5%-18.75%

for whole life, term and endowment is given by percentage for EMRs ranging from +25 to +125 for different age groups.

Corresponding Premium increase of different plans to different EMRs

General range of percentage increase for whole life, endowment and term plans for only two age bands.[6]

Explanatory Example

Ram is 25 years old. His extra mortality is 100%. Extra premium for various plans for Ram will be as follows:

Term plan = Premium Rs. 1000

Rated Premium* = 100% × 1000 = Rs. 2000

Endowment Plan = Premium Rs. 4000

Range of Rated Premium** = 10 to15% × 4000 = Rs. 4400 to 4600

Whole life Plan = Premium Rs. 3000

Range of Rated Premium*** = 25% to 35% × 3000 = Rs. 3750 to 4050

Notes :

* In case of term plan the premium has doubled but for other plans the increase has been less.

** As per table of endowment above for ages between 21 to 30 years for 100% EMR the range of premium increase is between 10 to 15%.

*** As per table of whole life above for ages between 21 to 30 years for 100% EMR the range of premium increase is between 25 to 35%.

Unit Linked Insurance Plans (ULIPs) is another very popular plan being sold today. It is a combination of a risk coverage (term plan) component and an investment portion. The proportion of coverage and investment is decided by the applicant and any rating that results from underwriting assessment is imposed on the risk coverage portion of the premium. Description of ULIP plans is given in Annexure 8.

RATINGS OF DISCLOSED MEDICAL CONDITIONS

The ratings of medical conditions in the underwriting manual are prepared over a period of time by reinsurers[7] using mortality experience, information on medical and clinical trials and some general population studies. The 1983 Medical

Impairment Study of USA, gives a comparison, based on authentic volumes of data for many impairment groups. In this study comparison is made with a similar study of 1951 which shows changes in mortality experience and reflects changes in underwriting standards.

The extra mortality rates (EMR) for various diseases and conditions are given in this chapter. These vary from life insurance company to company based on the specific underwriting manual that each follows. Insurance companies do not publish their underwriting guidelines, as intermediaries and agents may take unfair advantage of them. Therefore, the ratings shown in this chapter are a blend of general indicative ratings.[8] Here it needs mention that EMR of 300% or more is usually declined by the underwriters. This has been discussed later in this chapter.

Overweight

Being overweight or obese puts a strain on the body's systems, for example the heart has to work harder to pump the blood around the body. Obesity, therefore, can lead to raised blood pressure and may cause coronary artery disease. The overweight person can also fall prey to diabetes as well as minor disorders such as hernias and varicose veins. An individual's built—the relationship between height, weight, and girth—is one of the basic factors to assess mortality expectation. During the late 19th century and early 20th century comprehensive statistical studies were done on the relationship between body mass, blood pressure and mortality experience on life insurance policies issued by leading insurance companies. The findings of these studies as refined and supplemented by subsequent investigations, served as the basis for the 'built tables' used by life insurance companies for several decades. These tables did allow for some obesity. Some life insurance companies do have more generous EMRs for obesity than others. A client who is heavier than the built table given weight may still be acceptable at standard rates, if there are no other adverse features. When a client is considerably overweight, the company may request an MER even if the case is non-medical. Most applicants understandably, overstate their height and understate their weight, and so the MER may reveal that a 55 kg female is really 65 kg. The medical examiner informs the underwriter of the client's weight and records complications of being overweight, if any. Clients who are underweight are generally acceptable at standard rates. But an MER may be requested to ascertain if there is a reason associated to his being underweight such as a history of TB, anorexia nervosa or AIDS.

TABLE 6.4

Age less than 34	**EMR**
BMI 29 to 30	+25
BMI 31 to 32	+50
BMI 33 to 34	+75
BMI 35 to 36	+100
BMI 37 to 39	+150
BMI 40 to 41	+200
BMI 42 to 43	+250
BMI 44 and above	Likely decline
Age 35 to 54	
BMI 29 to 30	+25/std
BMI 31 to 32	+25/std
BMI 33 to 34	+25/+50
BMI 35 to 36	+50
BMI 37 to 39	+75/100
BMI 40 to 41	+125
BMI 42 to 43	+150
BMI 44 and above	Individual assessment based on other risk factors
Age 55 to 69	
BMI 29 to 30	Std
BMI 31 to 32	Std
BMI 33 to 34	Std
BMI 35 to 36	+25
BMI 37 to 39	+50/+75
BMI 40 to 41	+75/+100
BMI 42 to 43	+100
BMI 44 and above	Individual assessment based on other risk factors

Std = Standard.

In underwriting manual for obesity the EMRs are given in terms of Body Mass Index (BMI). It is a measure of body fat based on height and weight. BMI is defined as the individual's body mass divided by the square of the height, and is almost always expressed in the unit kg/m^2. It may be noted that the EMR also depends on the age of an applicant. With younger applicants rated more conservatively than older ones. Therefore, the EMR will be lower for an older applicant than that for a young applicant with the same BMI. The reason for this is that for older ages the actuaries have already accounted for some degree of mortality in the standard premium rates and accordingly the premium rates are kept higher for older people. There is therefore no need to rate up older people to the same degree as for younger persons for overweight.

When the BMI of a client is above 33, there might be other medical conditions which are present such as high blood pressure, high blood sugar, raised liver enzymes or raised cholesterol levels, etc.

The effect of two or more factors like high blood pressure and overweight is not always additive (the two loadings are simply not added up). The effect of these factors can be cumulative. For example the underwriter may give a +100 EMR when the sum of EMR of overweight is +25 and high blood pressure is +50 even though the total of the two ratings comes to +75. This is done due to the fact that the effect of two risk factors is exponential in some cases. When dealing with clients with multiple problems the complexity of underwriting gets considerably accentuated.

Diabetes Mellitus (Diabetes)

Diabetes mellitus occurs when the pancreas does not produce enough insulin for the body's need. Diabetes is not curable. The standard treatment for diabetes is to control it by regular injections of insulin combined with a strict regime of diet. In some cases, control can be achieved by diet alone or in combination with oral drugs. With regular treatment and precautionary measures, a diabetic can often lead a normal lifestyle. Poor control of the blood sugar can lead to coma (which are brought about by excessive presence of insulin or too little intake of food), general deterioration (leading to other metabolic disorders), damage to blood vessels/retina/kidney or damage to nervous and cardiovascular systems. It is regrettable that many diabetics do not follow their diet schedules or comply with prescribed treatment.

An MER with a diabetic questionnaire gives the history of the disease. MER is also necessary to ascertain other complications such as eye disorders, hypertension and excessive sugar in the urine. Effectively, there are two types of diabetes viz. Type I and Type II. More favorable of the two is maturity-onset diabetes (Type II diabetes).[9] Although it is generally found in the middle-aged and elderly people it can occur at younger ages also. It is often discovered in overweight persons and may be controlled by diet alone.

Normal blood sugar level in a person is recognized by medical science at 65 to 109 milligrams per deciliter of blood. If the sugar in the blood goes higher than this threshold it is recognized as diabetic condition. The usual blood test that picks this up in a life insurance medical examination is the Fasting Blood sugar test. The life span of a diabetic can greatly increase if his blood sugar is kept near normal. Insurance companies are very keen to find out if the diabetic client's blood sugar remains in the level of 100 to 130 which is considered a decent control of the disease. Since clients may take medications like insulin to lower their blood sugar before an insurance medical test another test called HbA1c is sometimes asked for by the underwriters to see the control of blood sugar in past 3 months.

An underwriter assigns great importance to the level of blood sugar control. The risk of most organ damage (diabetic complications) increases as the blood sugar rises. Diabetics do not die from diabetes per se but from its complications. The various complications that can occur in a diabetic person are stroke, eye disorders, peripheral blood vessels (gangrene etc.), heart attacks (risk of heart attack in diabetic patient increases two-fold) and renal diseases.

To rule out the existence of any of these resultant infirmities in a diabetic client underwriters sometimes ask for an eye examination, Treadmill ECG test and urine analysis (to assess kidney function). The following table gives a good idea of how an underwriter assesses a diabetic case and how he arrives at the EMR. The importance given to factors such as age at the time of diagnosis, years since diagnosis, control of sugar, smoking habits, protein in urine (indicator of kidney damage) etc., need to be noted.

TABLE 6.5
Age at the Time of Application (of a Diagnosed Diabetic)

Less than 16	*Opinion of the Chief Medical Officer (CMO) sought (usually declined)*
17 to 29	+150
30 to 49	+100
50 to 59	+75
60 to 69	+ 50
70 to 79	+ 25
More than 80	Standard
Duration Since diabetic	
Less than 5 years	No addition rating to the above mentioned
6 to 15 years	Add upto +25
More than 15 year	
If no complications and age more than 60	No additional rating
Otherwise	Add +25 or +50
Control and Compliance	
Optimal Control of blood sugar (below 125 mg/dl)	Reduce rating by 50
Average Control of blood sugar	No additional rating
Poor control of blood sugar (serious doubts about compliance to medical advise)	+50 or +100 or even decline depending on blood sugar
Urine Analysis	
Proteinuria (protein in urine)	
Less than 2 mg	No additional rating
Trace or + (microalbuminuria)	Add + 50 or +100
2+ or 3+	Add +150 on advise from CMO
4+	Decline
Ketones in Urine	Postpone case

Neuropathy Nerve Complication)	Decline
Renal Disease	Decline
Retinopathy (Eye complications)	Decline
Hypertension	Add rating according to hypertension table
Hypertension with Proteinuria	Decline
Increased Cholesterol with Proteinuria	Decline
Smoking	
Smoking with No Proteinuria	+25/+50 for less than 20 cig /day
	Decline if more than 20 cig/day
Smoking with Proteinuria	Decline
Obesity	Add rating
Heart (ECG) Abnormalities	Decline

Maturity-onset diabetes is frequently found in Asians. Insulin-dependent diabetes is generally more severe and, provided there are no other complications the applicant is insurable. EMRs for this variant of diabetes are much higher and depend on the degree of blood sugar control and additional complications.

Generally, it is found that the Medical Examination report first reveals the presence of sugar in the urine and the possible presence of diabetes in life insurance applicants. Complications such as obesity and hypertension increase the loadings and may lead to denial of life insurance. Generally, the longer a person has diabetes the more likely he is to suffer from the resultant complications and other associated illnesses. Hence the ratings are highest for the younger applicants who have already had the disease for 10 years or more. The reasons for diabetes are unknown but the predisposing factors include family history of diabetes (that is the parents having the disease), overweight, smoking, high blood pressure, etc.

Hypertension (High Blood Pressure)

Hypertension (High blood pressure) may be a symptom of a condition that impairs longevity. It is particularly associated with kidney ailments. A combination of overweight and hypertension is always regarded as a serious health hazard. Low blood pressure can usually be disregarded unless it is abnormally low or associated with some definite impairment, such as tuberculosis or congestive heart failure. High blood pressure that responds to treatment by returning to normal levels may receive favorable underwriting consideration, provided normal blood pressure levels are maintained and the other parameters such as weight and blood sugar are within normal limits.

Next to overweight, the most common reason for rating up is hypertension or high blood pressure. It is the manifestation of the increase in the pressure of blood in the large blood vessels of the body. Most people would remember having got their blood pressure checked at one time or the other with the doctor binding a pneumatic cloth over the arm and measuring the pressure through a device that has a mercury meter. As mentioned earlier, the blood pressure is measured both at the maximum pressure and the minimum pressure. Maximum blood pressure is called systolic and minimum is called diastolic. 120/80 reading is expressed as the normal blood pressure, i.e. 120 is the systolic and 80 is the diastolic blood pressure. The systolic blood pressure can change due to stress or emotion. Thus diastolic pressure is considered to be a better measure of the constant strain on the heart. (Systolic pressure is the higher pressure created by heart contractions, and the diastolic pressure is the residual pressure created by blood in the body without the added pressure of a heart contraction).

Insurance business experience indicates that both factors (systolic and diastolic) should be taken into consideration. If both are higher than normal, the mortality rate will be greater than if only one of the two is out of line. The reason for the increase of blood pressure in the body is because the blood vessels of the body get thickened and the heart has to exert more pressure in pumping blood through them. The blood vessels get thickened due to many factors. Common among them is the increasing age, obesity (overweight), smoking, excessive salt in diet, alcohol abuse, stress, diabetes, increased cholesterol levels, etc. Certain studies have found that obesity as a reason for hypertension in 70% of the individuals.

Hypertension is rated by underwriters due to various complications in the body that increase the risk of death and reduce life span. Hypertension if not controlled leads to damage to heart, damage to peripheral blood vessels, eye damage, brain vessels damage(stroke) and kidney damage. Fortunately blood pressure if controlled within normal range, through medication, reduces these risks substantially. Therefore, the life insurance underwriters always focus on the control of blood pressure in clients that have been diagnosed as hypertensive. It is important for the life insurance agents to tell the client who is hypertensive that the loading will depend on the current blood pressure that will be measured at the time of the insurance medical test. If the client has been following a good diet control with regular medical treatment, the rating may be very minimal. If the blood pressure is very high then the underwriter may suspect that the uncontrolled blood pressure has affected other organs of the body and may either ask for other tests such as ECG, Echo cardiograph (to assess heart), renal function tests (to assess kidneys) and then depending on the results of the test decide on the loading.

Applicants who are diagnosed for hypertension usually have to answer a written questionnaire regarding their medication. In such cases the underwriter's decision will be based on both the present level of blood pressure and the health of other body organs.

A hypertensive individual should take care that on the date of the medical examination he does not take coffee or cigarettes as these tend to increase the blood pressure. The blood pressure is taken thrice during the MER and the underwriter looks at an average of the three readings to rate the premium. If a hypertensive individual is on medicines and his blood pressure is controlled, and he has no other adverse factors such as smoking, overweight, cholesterol, blood sugar the underwriter generally will give standard rates on the case.

Thus even if a client is a diagnosed hypertensive he may be able to get standard rates if his other factors are favorable. If a client who does not know he has high blood pressure and during the medical examination the doctor discovers that the client has high blood pressure the underwriter may either charge extra premium and issue the policy or postpone the case depending on the level of high blood pressure that was measured.

In very high blood pressure cases instead of charging a very high extra premium the underwriter may postpone the case for 3 months so that the client may take treatment and then apply again for insurance. In case the blood pressure is then controlled the applicant may be able to get a better rating. The following table shows the EMR for the blood pressure detected during the medical test in an individual irrespective of whether the client has already been diagnosed for hypertension and is taking medicine for it.

Approximate rating for Hypertension is given below.

TABLE 6.6

BP	130/ 92	145/ 92	160/92	170/92	180/92	190/92
Rating	Standard	Standard	+50	+100	+150	Decline
BP	130/ 100	145/ 100	160/100	175/100	180/100	190/100
Rating	CMO	+25	+50	+100	+200	Decline
BP	130/110	145/110	160/110	175/110	180/110	190/110
Rating	CMO	+100	+175	+200	+250	Decline
BP	130/120	145/120	160/120	175/120	180/120	190/120
Rating	CMO	Decline	Decline	Decline	Decline	Decline

Abbreviation: CMO = Chief Medical Officer.

Smoking

Clinical tests and statistics show that smoking in particular is associated with lung cancer and has a high incidence in many other organ cancers. In addition, smoking is associated with a greatly increased risk of heart disease, respiratory disease and hypertension. Some life insurance companies do not differentiate between smokers and nonsmokers and work out their premium rates on aggregate rates. A few life insurance companies have introduced smoking differentials especially for term insurance. A discount of 30% may be available to non-smokers. EMRs mentioned below are applicable for an aggregate table of rates for smokers.

EMR for Smoking (For aggregate rates)

- 10-20 cigarettes a week +25 if no other risk factors are present.

If any other risk factor is present then the EMR is increased according to those factors

- 20-40 cigarettes a week +75 if no other risk factors are present*

Substandard Insurance—Reconsideration of Rating

To cater for the higher death rates that will certainly occur within the substandard group, the company collects an extra premium *from all* who are prone to the extra risk since it is not known which of the members of the group will contribute for the extra mortality rates. Obviously not every member of the group will die early or have a shorter life span than the normal life expectancy. However, a larger proportion of people in the substandard group will have a shorter life expectancy.[10]

If a policy holder's health improves he would want the insurance company to reduce or remove the rating. The insurance company do not remove or reduce the rating as at the time the policy was originally issued, the insured was placed in a special classification of risks where members are unhealthy to approximately the same degree. It is known to the life insurance companies that some of the members of the group would die within a short period, while others would survive far beyond their normal expectancy. It is also known that the health of some of the members would deteriorate with the passage of time, while of some other members would not. During the time the insured under consideration is in normal health, the health of many others in his original group would have markedly worsened. Many of them cannot now get insurance on any terms, while others are insurable only at a greater extra

* The application can be declined if this kind of smoking is present in conjunction with diabetes and the rating can be doubled if heavy smoking present in conjunction with high blood pressure and increased cholesterol levels in addition to the rating for the respective conditions.

premium than what was charged initially. If the company reduces the premiums for those whose health has improved, it should be permitted to increase the premiums of those whose health has deteriorated. Because the premiums for those whose health has deteriorated cannot be increased, the premiums of those whose health has improved should not be reduced.

Sometimes the applicants request the removal of rating on a case where an extra premium has been imposed on account of occupation or residence hazards. In such cases if the insured is no longer in a high risk occupation or high risk residence location, the rating and the corresponding extra premium is discontinued. Here it is necessary to take care of the possibility that the insured may subsequently return to the hazardous occupation or residence, or that his or her health has already been affected adversely. For such policies some life insurance companies require that a specified period of time, such as one or two years, must elapse after leaving the hazardous occupation or risk prone residence location before the rating is removed. Occasionally, a medical examination is also required along with adequate proof of change of occupation or residence.

MEDICAL REJECTION

Certain diseases render applicants ineligible for life insurance policies. Diseases with high extra mortality rates of +350 or more such as cancer, coronary artery disease, AIDS, etc. can be rejected permanently (declined) by insurance companies. People with these diseases are deemed "medically uninsurable." Risk factors, such as uncontrolled high blood pressure, are also a basis for rejection (postponed temporarily till the high blood pressure is controlled through medication). The rationale is that people with these diseases and risk factors have a very high probability of early death. If they die prematurely, they will not pay enough money in premiums to cover the losses that they will generate, unless the insurer were to charge them the extra premium based on EMRs of +300 or above which in many cases would make the insurance unaffordable. "Insurance is about sharing risks within a community. Underwriting is about exclusion. The industry term "uninsurable" as applied to people deemed to be at very high risk suggests that insurability is a quality of individuals. In fact, insurability is the set of policy decisions by insurers about those whom insurance is to be allowed. It is not a trait, but a concept of *membership*. It expresses the criteria used by a group to decide whom to include and whom to exclude from its redistributive system."[11]

There are some conditions which can cause decline or postponement of client's applications. These conditions are discussed in the following paragraphs. The list of these conditions is not exhaustive, only common conditions have been mentioned here.

Postponement of Cases

The following are common causes for postponement of cases applied for insurance on account of controllable impairments.

Diabetes: Very high blood sugar (above 150 mg/dl), detected for the first time at the time of insurance medical examination, is usually postponed. The case can be considered favorably and offered a better rate after 3-6 months when the client has taken medication and his or her blood sugar levels have improved.

High Blood Pressure: More than 170/100 mmHg is postponed if it is detected for the first time and also if it is an already diagnosed case on treatment. The client is advised to take treatment and if he comes back with lower blood pressure after 3 to 6 months the case is assessed again.

Tuberculosis: A person suffering from Tuberculosis is not offered any insurance although a fully treated tuberculosis case can be offered standard rates on proof of diagnosis, treatment and medical tests to establish current standard health.

Malignant tumors: Most people with malignant tumors are not insured for 4 years after completion of treatment as statistics show that mortality during this period is very high. After a period of 4 years the individuals may be insured with a rating depending upon the type and extent of the tumor.

Heart Bypass: A person with a Heart Bypass or angioplasty surgery cannot be insured within 1 year from the date of the surgery.

Very high liver enzymes: Detection of very high levels liver enzymes in an apparently healthy and asymptomatic person is one of the common yet confusing causes of postponement for clients and agents. The liver enzymes can be raised for a variety of reasons and it is difficult for the underwriter to determine the reason for the raised enzymes as also whether it is a serious cause or otherwise. Therefore, most underwriters take the wait and watch approach and postpone the case for 3 months after which a fresh assessment of the case is made.

Chest X-Ray Abnormality: The chest X-ray is not a very sophisticated medical diagnostic test. An abnormality on the chest X-ray usually requires further tests to identify the exact problem. Underwriters always have to take a decision of a case in a cost effective manner. They usually postpone the case rather than requesting for advanced medical test like CT or MRI which are fairly expensive. They hope that the clients will get the test done at their own expense and get back to the company later with the report so that they can evaluate the case at a later date at a less expense.

Decline Cases on Account of Serious Impairments

In mature markets some companies do not decline any case. They rate the case up as per the risk which in some cases makes the insurance unaffordable to the client. In India most companies have a threshold of +350 EMR in medical cases beyond which they decline the case. So if client's medical factors indicate that his EMR is +375 they would decline the case rather than give him such a high rated up premium which would essentially be unaffordable.

The following conditions carry very high risk with it and, therefore, client's with these conditions find their applications declined.

Diabetes

- With an abnormal (positive) ECG exercise
- Diabetes with Albumin in urine
- Diabetes with complications of other organs

Hypertension

- Very high Blood Pressure associated with proteinuria.

Tumors Recently Diagnosed or in Treatment

- Leukemia
- Breast Cancer

Other Diseases

- Systemic Lupus Erythematosus (SLE)
- Coronary Artery Disease (CAD) below 40 years of age
- Paralysis
- Ulcerative colitis
- Polycystic kidney
- Cirrhosis of liver
- Alzheimer's disease
- Organ transplant recipient (In certain rare cases kidney transplant recipient is given a policy with high rating if current health condition is good)
- Chronic pancreatitis
- Acquired immune deficiency syndrome (AIDS)
- Cystic fibrosis
- Muscular dystrophy
- Renal failure

When the application for insurance is declined or postponed it causes concern and anxiety both to the client and the agent. While the client is worried about his health, the agent loses his credibility and business. While agents are not kept informed about the reason of decline or postponement, many times insurance companies do not give any explanation to the clients and may only inform their family doctors. Some standard regulation is very much required in this area to ensure that the insurance seeking public is not kept in dark about some potentially serious medical condition that has been detected through insurance medical examination.

Many life insurance underwriters work on the principle that it is better to be safe than sorry. For them it is easier to decline than accept. However, with the increase in business competition, availability of more robust data pool and pressure from the market, the percentage of rejected life insurance cases will continue to decrease. In the liberalized Indian insurance market over the last 5 years, it is seen that companies are slowly relaxing their underwriting policy in areas such as the non-medical limits and ratings for certain risk aspects of health like family history and obesity. As long as companies expand their market and gain favorable claims, this trend will continue. In fact there will be more people who will be insured under substandard category than earlier as many individuals who were declined insurance earlier may be able to get insurance albeit at a higher premium rate. Substandard insurance is of great social importance because it makes insurance protection available to millions of families that would otherwise be without it.

Notes and References

1. Reflections-RGA's Medical Underwriting Newsletter, Volume 16, Spring 2006, Crediting Programs—"Giving Credit, Where Credit is Due" by J. Carl Holowaty, M.D.
2. Underwriting—A Dying Art? by T.S. Leigh, F.I.A., F.C.I.I. (Presented to the Institute of Actuaries, 26 March 1990).
3. Insurance Underwriting: A Managerial Perspective, Vol. III, 2002, ICFAI University Press.
4. Annexure 8 has details about different types of insurance plans.
5. Underwriting—A Dying Art? by T.S. Leigh, F.I.A., F.C.I.I. (Presented to the Institute of Actuaries, 26 March 1990).
6. Annexure 9 has corresponding extra premium for EMRs 25 to 125 for ages 21 to 60 years.
7. Reinsurers take on part of the risk that insurers assume from their clients.
8. Underwriting—A Dying Art? by T.S. Leigh, F.I.A., F.C.I.I. (Presented to the Institute of Actuaries, 26 March 1990).
9. Type 1 diabetes mellitus—formerly known as insulin-dependent diabetes (IDDM), childhood diabetes, is characterized by loss of the insulin-producing beta cells of the islets of Langerhans of the pancreas leading to a deficiency of insulin. It should be noted that there is no known preventative measure that can be taken against type 1 diabetes. Most people affected by type 1 diabetes are otherwise healthy and of a healthy weight when onset occurs. Diet and exercise cannot reverse or prevent type 1 diabetes. Diabetes mellitus type 2 (formerly called diabetes mellitus type II, non-insulin-dependent diabetes (NIDDM), obesity-related diabetes, or adult-onset diabetes) is a metabolic disorder that is primarily characterized by insulin resistance, relative insulin deficiency,

and hyperglycemia. It is presently incurable. It is rapidly increasing in the developed world, and there is some evidence that this pattern will be followed in much of the rest of the world in coming years. Genetic factors, usually polygenic, are present in most patients. However, environmental factors such as obesity, lack of exercise and a sedentary lifestyle are thought by most observers to lead to insulin resistance. Certainly not all type 2 diabetics have a family history of the condition.

10. McGill's Life Insurance, Fifth Edition, Edward E. Graves, Editor, Lynn Hayes, Managing Editor, The American College Press, 2004.
11. AIDS and the Moral Economy of Insurance By Deborah Stone, The American Prospect Online Edition.

PART III

FUTURE OF UNDERWRITING

Chapter 7

New Frontiers

The material in this chapter should enable the reader to understand

- Role of genetics in Underwriting
- Underwriters as risk managers
- New concepts of underwriting, tele-underwriting and automated underwriting

CHAPTER

New Frontiers

GENETIC TESTING AND ITS IMPACT ON UNDERWRITING

Fair Discrimination in Underwriting

Medical underwriting involves assessing the applicant's risk of sickness or death. For this purpose applicants are grouped together into risk classes and charged premiums relative to the risk class they belong to. A person in a higher risk class is charged higher premium, while a person in a lower risk class is charged a lower premium. Based on personal risk factors applicants are classified into three risk classes, viz. standard, substandard, or declined. A person with a standard rating would have a lower premium than a person with a substandard rating and while some applicants with uninsurable risk factors may be refused insurance altogether. Laws allow insurance companies to discriminate among applicants through risk classification. Statutorily and commercially, risk classification is considered "fair" discrimination. Fair discrimination entails those risks where it can be demonstrated that a particular risk causes a variation or deviation from actual or reasonably anticipated result. In demonstrating this relationship, the actuary of the insurance company may use relevant information from any reliable source, including statistical or other mathematical analysis of available data. The actuary may also take aid of clinical experience and expert opinion. If differences in rates reflect material differences in expected cost for risk characteristics, then, for the purposes of risk classification differential rates are considered equitable. "Unfair discrimination" in the context of life insurance is "that which treats individuals of the same class and equal expectation of life differently." Conversely, unequal treatment of insureds who fall in different risk classifications is "fair" discrimination.

Anti-selection

The underwriting or risk selection and classification process can be fair only when the underwriter knows as much about the applicant's risk as the applicant does himself. However, there maybe situations when there is an un-level playing field, and the applicant knows more about his risk than the insurer does and the applicant does not disclose this information in the application form. This phenomenon is known as 'anti-selection' or 'adverse selection'.

The underwriting process is geared to limit 'anti-selection' as the underwriters' can access physicians, employers, and all other sources relevant to the insurance contract, in order to classify risk accurately. The advent of genetic testing has created a situation which could harm both the life insurer and the applicant. On one hand, life insurers might use genetic information obtained from testing to practice unfair discrimination, on the other hand, applicants might withhold their genetic information from life insurers, resulting in anti-selection.[1]

Pros and Cons of using genetic information for underwriting

Genetic testing is the genetic diagnosis of vulnerabilities to inherited diseases. It can also be used to determine a person's ancestry. Each person carries two copies of every gene, one inherited from his mother and the other inherited from his father. The human genome is believed to contain about 25,000 genes. In addition to studying chromosomes to the level of individual genes, genetic testing in a broader sense also includes biochemical tests for the presence or absence of key proteins. These key proteins signal aberrant versions of certain genes which are used to find changes that are associated with inherited disorders. Results of a genetic test can confirm or rule out a suspected genetic condition or help determine a person's chance of developing or passing on to offspring the genetic disorder. Modern genetic knowledge has made possible hundreds of genetic tests for collecting health information and many more are being developed.[2] For underwriters genetic information will become very helpful as and when genetic testing techniques become more commercially available and accessible.

There may always be a possibility that those who are at risk for genetic diseases and have knowledge of it may withhold this information from insurers to avoid being classified as substandard or being denied life insurance by the insurance companies. This tendency leads to a potential for anti-selection.

Such anti-selections make the underwriting process falter since risk classification becomes less accurate. Life insurers, therefore, believe that they should have access to genetic information because if insurers are not entitled to the genetic information known to the applicant, anti-selection may become more prevalent and the complete life insurance process may get vitiated. If anti-selection is not kept in check it leads to an increase in claims which results in losses for the life insurance companies.

The other issue pertaining to the access to genetic information by insurance companies is the concerns of privacy. Genetic information is regarded as private information. Once an individual is genetically tested, the result gives a blueprint of that individual's genetic makeup which can be used to trace genes through past generations. Genetic blueprint predicts the likelihood of the gene's presence in living generations, and can also be used to predict their presence in future generations. Obtaining someone's genetic information could lead to finding genetic disorders for that person's parents, siblings, and children. Such information becomes a matter of concern if insurers discover a genetic disorder in one person, and they use that information to classify related persons as well.

Access to genetic test results, do also have a variety of positive effects for the insured apart from reducing anti-selection phenomena. Early genetic diagnosis allows the applicant the opportunity to make better-informed choices, that is, changes in lifestyle and preventive intervention potentially leading to a better prognosis.

Another question to understand is whether risk classification, based on genetic information, is actuarially 'fair discrimination'. While it can be argued that the use of genetic information for life insurance underwriting purposes is not new. Insurers have been collecting information about an applicant's family history for decades. But the public fear of misuse of genetic information is not unfounded either. Thus the issue of genetic information availability to the insurers needs well thought of regulations and codes of conduct.[3]

AUTOMATED UNDERWRITING AND TELE-UNDERWRITING

Automated Underwriting

Life insurance companies always look for fast, efficient and cost effective ways for processing life insurance applications. Lower staff costs, greater accuracy and better consistency are the coveted goals of life insurance underwriters. A quicker turnover using computerized systems for underwriting helps in achieving these goals. If the life insurance application form is completed satisfactorily, acceptance follows automatically through a computerized system. The client thus does not have to wait for days as the application is accepted almost instantly. The method used by these computer programs basically involves the input of critical pieces of information on the life insurance application form. These are then evaluated according to a set of rules which are programmed into the computer, e.g. acceptable height and weight ratios, or which all medical conditions can be ignored. The system however, is not foolproof, as wrong feeding of information could defeat the purpose for which a program is created. But a robust automated system can help an insurance company save considerable time and manpower costs by underwriting majority of the cases especially in the non-medical category. For medical category applications also systems can be devised which can ensure that all automated requirements (MER, etc.) have been punched and key findings have been entered before the case is sent for human underwriting. Automated underwriting does have limitations as computers are capable of only making logic-based decisions, whereas underwriting entails an element of judgment which is beyond the logic-based decisions. Human underwriters thus will always be needed to define and assess the risks. Nevertheless, as computer systems advance more and more, many parameters may be covered under computer programs leaving only a small percentage of cases which will need human underwriters. Underwriters, none the less will continue to set the pace, theme and trail for the computer systems.[4]

Tele Underwriting

In traditional underwriting process the underwriter captures data from the application forms to assess and evaluate the risk. Tele-underwriting also has the same methodology viz. to obtain accurate and complete medical information about the applicant. The tele-underwriting process involves a trained professional (underwriter or scripted caller) who calls the applicant and records the medical data exactly as given by the applicant on a telephone line. In contrast the traditional underwriting process does not involve any interaction between the underwriter and the applicant. Tele-underwriting, therefore, has some advantages like improved service and lower cost as the underwriting process commences immediately instead of waiting for several days until the application arrives on the underwriter's desk through mail. Other benefits of tele-underwriting process are reduction in paperwork and improved customer service on account of accurate records. On the qualitative side, the tele-underwriting process has seen success for around eight years now since it has been put to use around the world. There has been no negative impact on the number of claims on companies using the tele-underwriting system. In fact some companies have reported a reduction in the claims ratio after implementation of tele-underwriting.

The success of tele-underwriting can be attributed to two main factors. Firstly, applicants are more forthcoming and direct with their personal medical history when contacted on telephone by a trained medical professional than when they are dealing with the agent. Customers can be hesitant to discuss personal medical history face to face with an agent, who is often an acquaintance, friend, or a relative. But the answers provided to an anonymous medical professional over telephone tends to be without inhibition and consequently more accurate and more comprehensive. Secondly, agents may be constantly aware of the "right answers" needed to obtain standard rates and, therefore, may feel pressure to hurry through the medical questions, or even skip some questions.[5]

Effective questioning is the essence of an efficient tele-underwriting process. 'Drill-down' questions or detailed questioning of the aspects critical to underwriting cuts down on need for additional questionnaires and even medical tests in some cases. Though not very widely used in India currently, many companies in advanced countries who are looking at reducing costs and increasing efficiency in the underwriting process are using tele-underwriting.[6]

UNDERWRITERS AS RISK MANAGERS

The regular parameters of underwriting theory and practice, as comprehensively discussed in this book, fully bring out that the underwriters are at the core of the life insurance process. In olden days the underwriters selected the risks based on their experiential instincts. Now they heavily rely on the statistics based Extra Mortality Rates (EMRs) given in the underwriting manuals. The future shift, therefore, to automation and tele-underwriting, challenges the role of the underwriters in the life insurance business. The underwriters of the future, accordingly, have to adapt to the changes in the industry if they want to maintain their present prime status in life insurance industry. The knowledge, skills and experience of the underwriters will be the key deciding factors for their survival and future prospects in the life insurance industry.

Underwriting—Knowledge, Skills, Experience and Authority

There is no qualifying professional degree for becoming an underwriter. Unlike medical and legal professions where an MBBS degree gives the license to practice medicine and a LLB degree to practice at Bar an underwriting professional attains his recognition and credibility in the life insurance industry solely through his hard work, knowledge, skill and experience. The key skills required for a good underwriter are decision-making, organization and planning, good verbal and written communication, analytical mind, critical thinking and attention to details.

Most underwriters in private life insurance companies are either people from medical or paramedical field such as doctors, nurses or pharmacists. Commerce and business graduates are also hired for assessing financial risks. Life insurance companies train commerce and business graduates on the medical underwriting aspects as an underwriter must be well versed with both medical and financial risks evaluation. People hired from the medical background are given on the job training to enable them to underwrite cases involving financial risk analysis. Training of fresh hires generally goes on for a period of 6 months to a year before they are allowed to underwrite cases independently. The cases that they are allowed to underwrite initially are for small sums and for younger age group clients. As they gain confidence and experience they move on to more complex cases of higher sums assured.

The authority limit of an underwriter is the sum assured that an underwriter is allowed to take a decision. Experienced underwriters are allowed to take sole decisions on large sum assured cases. These cases not only require complex medical analysis but thorough understanding of financial documents such as balance sheets, profit/loss statements, etc. to assess the financial adequacy for life insurance purposes.

The underwriting department is usually headed by an experienced underwriter who has proven knowledge of medical and financial aspects of life insurance. The department head is supported by a Chief Medical Officer (CMO) for medical decisions, if the head is not a medical doctor. The decision making power and responsibility rest fully with the head of the underwriting department.

Each underwriter has full authority of taking decision on the case under his consideration. The decision can be reviewed only by the supervisors or the head of the department. Life insurance companies are well aware of the importance of underwriting and maintain the solemnity of the decision making process. Life insurance companies uphold the decision taken by the head of the underwriting department and consider it as final.

On the Threshold of Transition

Despite the fact that an underwriter is the back bone of life insurance business, the main role of underwriters as seen by the life insurance companies is to deliver quality business at low cost and with good expediency. This, to an extent, has resulted in making underwriting a mechanical process. Use of computers and tele-underwriting has furthered abated the intuitive aspects of the underwriting process. However, even with advanced computer programs, reliance on human underwriters' underwriting skills, judgment and insight using years of experience cannot be ignored. The future underwriting manager's competence consequently would lie in efficiently and effectively separating the routine cases that can be handled mechanically from the special ones needing human analysis.

The challenge before the life insurance industry, therefore, is to strike a balance between decision-making through a scientific reasoning and preserving underwriter's intuition and mystique necessary to limit moral hazards and anti-selection.[7] The future underwriters will need to play the role of a risk manager in the true sense. They will need to learn to use data to influence product design, manage the business and review the underwriting policy. Underwriters routinely are over dependant on medical reports and underwriting manuals. The matching of the medical condition to the EMR is one task that can be easily taken over by the computer. The underwriters of tomorrow will have to focus on analysis of underwriting practices, turn around times, costs per case, pipeline volumes and rated or declined cases ratios in order to make the underwriting process more viable and efficient. An important role of the future underwriters will also be to monitor medical evidence to analyze if medical tests actually brought in useful decision-making information keeping in view the cost factors of medical expenditure by product line and distribution channels on rated and declined cases.

The new liberalized life insurance market has thrown many other challenges for the underwriters. In the erstwhile monopolistic environment prior underwriting decision on an applicant could be traced and effectively used when he applied for insurance again. Now with so many companies operating in liberalized Indian insurance market there have been instances where an individual who is declined life insurance cover by one company applies to another company without disclosing any prior information and manages to get insured. In the absence of a central repository of rated or declined applications, as exists in some western countries, coping with non-disclosure of prior underwriting decisions will be one of the major problems for underwriters in the coming years. Another major problem will be underwriting for new products which are released for high risk groups, such as diabetics, etc., for which most of the life companies do not possess adequate clinical data. These and other new challenges will hopefully lead the underwriters to rise to new frontiers of technical and operational excellence.

Notes and References

1. Actuarial Standards Board, Actuarial Standard of Practice, No. 12, Risk Classification (for All Practice Areas), Revised Edition, Developed by the Task Force to Revise ASOP No. 12 of the General Committee of the Actuarial Standards Board Adopted by the Actuarial Standards Board, December 2005, Doc. No. 101.
2. *Source*: Website- http://en.wikipedia.org/wiki/Genetic_testing
3. Read A: Genetics and insurance. *Genetics Law Monitor* 2002.
4. Underwriting—A Dying Art? by T.S. Leigh, F.I.A., F.C.I.I. (Presented to the Institute of Actuaries, 26 March 1990).
5. The Impact of Tele-Underwriting on Mortality Experience, By Jonathan Crumiller, Chief Operating Officer & Tele-Underwriting Practice Leader, Spring 2006 Princeton Consultants, Tele Underwriting Practice.
6. T.S. Ramakrishna Rao, *IRDA Journal*, Oct. 06.
7. Peter Maynard, Taking the Art Out of Underwriting viewed on website http://www.allfinanz.com/

PART IV

LEGAL ASPECTS—SELECTED LIFE INSURANCE COURT CASES

CASE 1

LIFE INSURANCE CORPORATION OF INDIA VS. SMT. G.M. CHANNABASAMMA (1991) (1) SCC 357A (A CASE DECIDED BY THE SUPREME COURT OF INDIA)

This case illustrates the burden of proof on the insurance company in case a claim is denied. The insurance company's responsibility of thorough investigation at the time of underwriting through medical examination has also been highlighted. In this case, the implication of the incontestability clause case further emphasizes the role of thorough scrutiny at the time of application. The Insurance Act, 1938, Section 45 puts onus on the insurance company to prove fraudulent non-disclosure if the statements made by the insured are called in question by the insurer after the expiry of two years from the date on which the policy was effected.

Background and Facts of the Case

A legal Suit was filed by G.M. Channabasamma for realization of a sum of Rs. 77,805.85 due from four insurance policies held by her deceased husband T.R. Gurupadaiah. Life Insurance Corporation (LIC) denied the claim as the deceased was guilty of fraudulent misrepresentations and suppression of material facts with regard to his health while filling up the proposal forms (application forms) for the policies.

The four policies were taken out between July 30, 1959 and August 23, 1961. The insured died on October 14, 1961 in a hospital for tubercular patients. According to LIC the deceased was suffering from acute diabetes and disease of the lungs which he was fully aware of at the time of taking the policies and had fraudulently denied these facts in the proposal forms, LIC felt that the last policy was taken only two months before death and it cannot be believed that he did not know about his illness.

The trial court ruled in favour of LIC and the claimant appealed to the High Court which reversed the decision. LIC appealed to the Supreme Court where the following arguments were put forward.

Arguments

The wife of the deceased (claimant) contended that her husband died of tuberculosis but neither he nor any member of the family had any knowledge of his illness at the time of taking the policy. He was keeping good health and actively taking part in his business. The discovery of the disease which accounted for his early demise was made very late. The allegations of fraudulent misrepresentation and suppression of material fact were emphatically denied by the claimant.

The witnesses in this case were the doctors who had examined the insured at various stages during the last few years. Dr. M.S. Kumar who claimed to have treated Gurupadaiah from 1953 to 1957 deposed that he was giving Gurupadaiah injections of insulin, anacobia and vetabion and was examining his urine which contained sugar. This witness had been disbelieved by the High Court on ground of his enmity with Gurupadaiah's father-in-law G.B. Mallikarjunaih. In view of the inconsistency in the records which Dr Kumar produced to support his claim that he treated the insured and the dispute between the two the Supreme Court concluded that they could not rely on the evidence given by Dr. Kumar that Gurupadaiah was under his treatment at any time.

Another doctor Dr. H.N. Gangadhar was examined by the court. He was the family doctor of Mallikarjunaih and he denied that Gurupadaiah was his patient. He however, stated that he had given two injections to him (of anacobin) in October 1958 and November 1958. According to his evidence the injections are harmless and can be even given to healthy men as tonic and thus the court did not take this evidence as any conclusion of disease suffered by Gurupadaiah.

Dr. Siddalingaih the doctor in the TB hospital, where the insured died, stated that Gurupadaiah was admitted as indoor patient with severe cough trouble and chest pain. The doctor opinioned that the insured may have been ill for 6 months before his admission to the hospital however, on cross examination he accepted that if a man is weak and not in a position to resist infection then the tuberculosis symptoms may come within a month. This evidence could also not be treated as conclusion that the insured was inflicted by a serious disease for a long time.

The LIC doctors who had certified the good health of insured at the time of taking out the insurance policies and who were examined as defense witnesses, disproved the case of illness. It has not been suggested that these doctors were either won over by the insured or were negligent in performing their duty. They had submitted confidential reports about the health of the insured and were of the opinion that he was in good health.

Decision of the Court

The Supreme Court held that the burden of proof that the insured had made false representations and suppressed material facts was undoubtedly on the Life Insurance Corporation. They agreed with the High Court decision that the LIC had failed to discharge the burden of proving that the insured was seriously ill at the time of taking out the insurance policies and knowingly suppressing material information. LIC, accordingly was directed to pay out the assured sum to the claimant.

Comments

As can be seen from this case the medical examination at the time of underwriting becomes critical if a dispute arises at the time of claim regarding the health of the insured. It is not easy for the insurance company to prove misrepresentation when its own doctors have given a clean chit of good health to the insured at the time of applying for the policy.

CASE 2

MANOHAR LAL *vs.* LIFE INSURANCE CORPORATION OF INDIA AIR 1981 DEL 171 (A CASE DECIDED BY THE HIGH COURT OF DELHI)

This case highlights the value of occupation, status and nature of job in assessment of risk especially with regard to insurance on females. It gives a good understanding of the legal significance of 'material facts' as opposed to non-material information in filling up the application form. The case demonstrates the importance of the design of the contents of the application forms so as to include all relevant information because if a particular question is not asked in the application form the insured is not obliged to give that information. It also brings out some broad insurance law concepts which have bearing on underwriting.

Background and Facts of the Case

Manohar Lal took a joint policy* on his life and the life of his wife, Sita Rani on May 23, 1956 for a period of 25 years for a sum of Rs. 25,000. He paid the annual premium of Rs. 906.25. The terms of the policy were that in event of death of either of them before the date of maturity the sum assured was payable to the survivor. Sita Rani died on June 22, 1957. Manohar Lal

---

* Under a joint life plan two individuals are insured through one policy. It is a good plan for working couples or professionals offering financial security for both the lives. Incase of death of one of the policyholder the surviving partner gets the sum assured, the premium is stopped and on death of the surviving partner or maturity full sum assured along with bonus is paid back.

made a claim for the payment of the sum assured. LIC repudiated the claim on ground that there was fraudulent misrepresentation and that there was no valid contract of insurance on which a claim could be made. On March 22, 1960 the deceased's husband filed a claim in court of law against LIC for recovering Rs. 29, 125, i.e., the sum assured with the interest due on it.

Arguments

In its defense, LIC raised three points. The first was that the claimant did not disclose his occupation truthfully. LIC contended that in the proposal form the claimant had answered the question of 'profession and exact nature of duties' as 'tutor and photographer'. In his statement to the medical examiner on May 10, 1956 he had said that his occupation was 'private business'. In another personal statement on May 11, 1956 he had stated in reply to a similar question that his occupation was 'business'. LIC said that the above declarations regarding his occupation were misstatements because the investigation conducted by LIC showed that the claimant was in fact working as a 'laborer' in Birla Cotton Mills, Delhi at a monthly salary of Rs. 120. It was pleaded that the answers to the specific questions about occupation were 'material' for assessment of risk for a large sum of Rs. 25,000. The second ground was that the claimant's wife was observing 'purdah' (veil) while in her personal statement recorded on May 10, 1956 she had denied the same. The third point was that the claimant was not on good terms with his wife Sita Rani and he anticipated her early death and took the policy with a view to obtain money by her death. It was said that Manohar Lal had a meager income with which he could hardly continue the policy and he had precipitated the death of his wife Sita Rani. The contract of insurance was thus characterized as a wagering or gambling contract (speculative—because insurable interest did not exist) and therefore the life insurance policy was void and unenforceable in law.

With regard to the above pleas, for the misstatement regarding the purdah of Sita Rani, the Life Insurance Corporation's own witness, the insurance agent categorically stated that Sita Rani did not observe purdah. The court also refused to hold that the policy was obtained by Manohar Lal to gamble on his wife's life as LIC failed to give any worthwhile evidence that the couple had strained relations and that the claimant was instrumental in bringing about her early death. Sita Rani had contracted paratyphoid to which she succumbed after 12 days of illness.

The only other defense that needed consideration was the status and occupation of the claimant. The real question was whether non disclosure of his main occupation by claimant invalidated the insurance policy. It was established on record that Manohar Lal got employment at Birla Mills as an unskilled worker in 1950-51. He worked there in shifts as a machine man and was being paid according to the quantity of work he put in. His income was Rs. 125 per month. In April 1957 he left the mills to pursue photography. Two witnesses admitted that Manohar Lal was learning photography though it was not fetching him much income. Other witnesses stated that the claimant taught their sons or grandsons as a paid tutor after his shift hours at the Mills. LIC argued that the object to hide the information of his occupation by the claimant was to induce LIC to enter into a contract of insurance which it otherwise would have refused because 'the poverty of the person is itself a motive for committing fraud'. In other words Manohar Lal's sole disqualification was poverty which disentitled him from taking a policy of Rs. 25,000 though LIC agreed that they could have given him a policy for Rs. 5000. The court found this argument baseless as the LIC proposal form did not contain any question about the applicant's income or salary. Further, the evidence from a witness from the Mill showed that the claimant joined the Mill as a 'worker' and as a worker was entitled to wages, bonus, leave and security of employment.

Decision of the Court

The Court held that there was no fraud involved in the case as the claimant did not state any untruth and thus found the claim honest and just. As per the Insurance Act no contract shall be avoided by reason of inaccuracy of the statement unless it is material to the contract and the Court was of the view that there was no suppression of fact and the claimant never made any statement stating that he was a wealthy man. LIC's contention that the information about his income was 'material' could not be used as defense because it was never asked in the application. The policy was repudiated after more than two years by letter dated November 21, 1959. The burden under the Insurance Act Section 45 is on the insurer to show that suppression of facts was fraudulent and that the claimant knew at the time of making the statement of occupation that it was false. This could not be proved by the insurer and thus the Court passed a decree of Rs. 25,000 with interest of 6% per annum from date of suit till its realization with legal costs.

Comments

Such court cases have made insurance companies to carefully design their application forms to include all information that is critical for risk assessment by the underwriter. In cases where the underwriter finds vagueness or ambiguity in the answers given in the application form he should make further investigations so as to avoid likely legal battles.

CASE 3

SMT. KRISHNA WANTI PURI *vs.* LIFE INSURANCE CORPORATION OF INDIA AIR 1975 DEL. 19 (A CASE DECIDED BY THE HIGH COURT OF DELHI)

This case brings out the importance of various investigations which are used to verify different facts at the time of claim enquiry. It also highlights the avoidable loop holes related to medical examination at the time of issue of a policy.

Background and Facts of the Case

Dharam Pal Puri insured his life with LIC and took out four policies, first being on October 12, 1959. He died on 5th August 1964 and his widow claimed the sum assured on the four policies. The deceased was admitted to hospital on 4th August 1964 where it was recorded that he was suffering from Mitral Stenosis and auricular fibrillation which caused his death. LIC repudiated the claim on ground that Dharam Pal Puri was suffering from heart disease for many years and that he knew about his ailment at the time of taking the policies. He had fraudulently suppressed these facts and had not disclosed it in the application form that he was suffering from heart disease.

Arguments

The questions pertaining to general state of health and specific heart related questions were answered in negative by the insured in the application form. To prove the fraudulent concealment and material suppression of facts LIC examined three doctors Dr. Padmavati, Dr. V.K. Dewan and Dr. Santosh Singh, and obtained certificates from them which stated the medical condition of the deceased. Dr. Padmavati deposed in the court that the deceased had examined him in May and September 1959 and that he suffered from Mitral Stenosis and auricular fibrillation. She also said that the deceased was suffering from this disease since 1946 according to the statement made by him to her. She stated that she did not see the patient after September 1959. As regards the nature of the disease she said that the patient's case was a serious form of the disease and could be checked with a stethoscope by a general practitioner and did not require an electro cardiograph.

The other doctor Dr. Dewan attended to the deceased when he was admitted to the hospital on 4th August 1964. He stated that Dharam Pal Puri suffered from the very ailment that Dr. Padmavati mentioned for five to seven years before his death as told to him by his brother when he was admitted to the hospital.

Dr. Santosh Singh was the Registrar of the hospital where the deceased was admitted and also attended on him. Dr. Santosh Singh had signed two reports dated 31st October 1964, both of which stated that Dharam Pal Puri died as a result of heart failure. It also stated that the deceased was suffering for about 7 years before his death from the disease. Dr. Santosh Singh, later, on issued another certificate of hospital treatment dated 24th October 1964 and a report dated 28th November 1964 where he mentioned that a relative of the deceased had informed him that Dharam Pal Puri had been suffering from the disease only for last one year. The relative also produced another certificate allegedly signed by Dr. Santosh Singh which stated that the deceased had been suffering from the disease for the past 1.5 years. In the Court the conflicting reports given by Dr. Santosh Singh came under scrutiny. Dr. Santosh Singh said that he could not say which of these certificates were correct without referring to the original records of the hospital. The Court examined the records of the hospital and saw over writing on the records. The years of suffering from the ailment was altered in the records from 7.5 years written earlier to 1.5 years. Based on the evidence of these three doctors LIC lawyers urged in the Court that LIC was entitled to avoid all policies of

Dharam Pal Puri on grounds of fraud and suppression of material facts.

Smt. Krishna Wanti Puri's lawyers argued that Dr. Padmavati's statements should not be believed as the original hospital record could not be produced. The court did not disbelieve the testimony of Dr. Padmavati as she was a doctor of repute and had no motive to perjure herself. Also the Court was of the view that the production of original records at this stage could not be insisted upon since Dr. Padmavati saw the patient in 1959 and the court case took place in 1970. With the passage of time the records maintained by the hospital where she saw the patient were destroyed as a matter of routine practice.

The claimant's lawyers then argued that no reliance should be placed on the testimony of Dr. VK Dewan and Dr. Santosh Singh as they were never told by the deceased that he was suffering from heart trouble for the last seven years. The deceased was brought to the hospital in an unconscious state by his brother who gave his past medical history to the attending doctors.

The Court was of the opinion that the brother was the best person to give the past history to the doctors and what he stated was possibly true as at that moment he wanted to save the life of his brother and would tell the truth.

On examination of the two witnesses the brother of the deceased and the wife of the deceased both denied the prior medical history.

The claimant's lawyer lastly argued that before issuing insurance policy LIC had got the deceased examined by three doctors. All these three doctors appeared in the witness box on behalf of the corporation. They deposed that in their opinion the deceased was fit to be insured at the time of examination. The court took the view that this did not advance the case of the claimant as the terms of the policy made it clear that the statement of health in the application was the basis of contract. The Court found that Dharam Pal Puri had taken pains to conceal that he had been treated for this serious ailment by Dr. Padmavati when in fact he had been treated by her only a few months before he took the first policy dated October 12, 1959. This shows that the insured's fraudulent suppression of his true medical history had an important bearing in his obtaining the policies from LIC.

Decision of the Court

The court ruled that LIC was entitled to avoid policies on ground of fraudulent misrepresentation of material facts.

Comments

Underwriters must be careful in evaluating the medical examination reports rendered by the life insurance company's doctors at the time of application. They should correlate it with the facts and data available from other sources such as application form, agent's report, etc. Relying on the doctor's report blindly can cause errors in decision-making as some untruthful applicants can deceive the examining doctors and obtain a clean chit in the medical examination.

PART V

SAMPLE UNDERWRITING SOLUTIONS

SOLUTION 1

CASE OF FRACTURE BY FALL OF A YOUNG GIRL

On a bright Monday morning Underwriter Usha opens her first case for the day. This is a non-medical case. It seems to be a clean simple case which she thinks will take no time. The case is for Rs. 5 lacs which is the maximum that she can underwrite as per her authority limit.

Facts of the Case

- Name of insured—Meena. Age 18 years;
- Occupation—student, Proposed by father a clerk in municipal water department;
- Annual income of father Rs. 1 lac per annum
- Policy—endowment for 20 years for sum assured of Rs. 5 lacs
- Premium—Rs. 20000 per annum
- Premium is 20% of the fathers annual income (it is unusual for an individual to put 20% of his income into an insurance premium—that too for a dependant daughter)
- No insurance on siblings or mother, father has a Rs. 2 lac policy from LIC.
- Medical History of the proposed life insured-fracture in leg due to fall in house one year back.

What are the main areas of concern in underwriting this case and what should be Usha's decision?

Case Solution

As Usha looks carefully at the life insurance on the family

members, she notices that the father has a life insurance policy of Rs. 2 lacs from LIC. There is no insurance on the mother. The siblings who are 2 boys aged 10 and 12 years have no insurance either. Sudha first decides to reduce the sum assured to Rs. 2 lacs (the company guidelines state that a child can be given life insurance of only Rs. 2 lacs if parents and siblings are not adequately insured). But then she changes her mind. She observes that the girl's medical history answer states a fracture in leg due to fall in the house. An 18 year old girl can have a fall; it is not unusual but the fall in the house makes Sudha suspicious. She immediately decides on asking for a Medical Examination. The medical report comes in after a few days and her doubts are confirmed, the young girl has been on anti-depressants and the doctor has stated that the fall was in fact from the balcony and was a suicide attempt.

Usha decides to decline the case but she does not have the authority to decline cases. She recommends declining the case and hands it over to her supervisor who approves the decline decision.

SOLUTION 2

A JUVENILE CASE DECLINED

Nitish, an underwriter in Kalyan Life Insurance Company came across this case for assessment at the end of his days work on a Thursday afternoon. It was a juvenile case of just Rs. 100000 Sum assured.

Facts of the Case

- The father of the proposed insured—Salaried in a private company, designation was not mentioned.
- The salary of father—Rs. 60000 per annum.
- No insurance on the parents or the siblings.
- Medical History of proposed Insured—Kidney stone 2 years back removed successfully at government hospital as per reports attached.

What are the critical aspects for underwriting in this case? What decision should Nitish take?

Case Solution

This small Rs. 1 lac policy on the life of the boy to be insured, a male of 10 years of age with 2 other older siblings, did not, as per company guidelines require any cover on either parents or siblings. Nitish noticed that the child had a kidney problem 2 years back for which all medical reports were attached. Anticipating complexity, Nitish kept the case aside to discuss it with the company's Medical Office the next day.

On Friday morning, Nitish took the case to company's medical officer for discussion. The reports suggested that the child had renal stone which was removed successfully at a government hospital. The medical officer did not want to bother much about it but suggested that Nitish should consult his underwriting supervisor before accepting and issuing the policy. Nitish while discussing the case with the supervisor realized that while they could not decline the application without any basis, the areas of concern were the unknown designation of the father, the child's identification proof which was a 2 year old school record and the address of the family which pointed to a very low socio economic area.

The supervisor asked Nitish to call for current school attendance of the child and insurance details on the family members. The reply from the agent came in the following week. The child was not going to school for the last two years and there was no insurance on any member of the family. Nitish had doubts that a major health complication may be the reason for the insured not attending a school. The insurance agent's report confirmed Nitish's doubts. The case was consequently declined as an uninsurable case.

SOLUTION 3

FEMALE INSURANCE, ASPECTS OF HOUSEWIFE AND PROFESSIONAL WOMEN

Hiren Patel (life insurance agent) has known the business family of Desai's for years. Deepak Desai runs his ancestral handicrafts export business. He has applied for a life insurance policy of Rs. 50 lacs. He also applied for the life insurance policy for his wife Seema for the same sum. They have been married or two years. Seema is well educated lady but Hiren does not know her exact qualifications. He also does not ask her to mention her work in the Desai family charitable trust. He is optimistic that both cases will get issued at standard rates due to the affluent background of the proposed insureds and their good health.

Facts of the Case

- Deepak's policy gets issued for Rs. 50. lacs.
- Seema's policy has been reduced to Rs. 10 lacs (maximum amount the company offers to a non-earning woman).

Hiren is upset and does not want to spoil an old relationship with Desai family. What can he do to get Seema's policy issued for the amount applied for which is Rs. 50 lacs?

Case Solution

Hiren calls up the underwriter and tells him to look through the papers to see that Seema has almost Rs. 1 crore worth property in her name. The underwriter is curt and replies that Hiren should look through the life insurance policy norms which say the women with un-earned income such as house property or investments are given a life insurance policy maximum of Rs. 10 lacs only.

Hiren Patel wonders if the company can not make an exception for a rich, modern and well educated woman. He goes through his files and realizes that he has not stated Seema's exact qualification and details of her involvement in the Desai family charitable trust. He makes enquiries and finds out that Seema is a qualified dentist and she is involved in running the Desai charitable health clinic. He sends the underwriter a courteous note with a copy of Seema's educational documents and employment details. Consequently the agent manages to get the life insurance policy cover issued for Rs. 50 lacs for Seema.

SOLUTION 4

IMPORTANCE OF FAMILY HISTORY

Santosh's both parents are diabetic. They are above 65 years. Santosh is 40 years old. He does not smoke and is slightly overweight. His blood pressure is slightly above normal as per the medical examination report given by the doctor.

This case lands up on the desk of underwriter Mr. Beema Lekhak. He mulls over the case and gets into a deep thought as to how to rate it. The life insurance agents anticipation was that most likely the underwriter will not send the applicant for a blood sugar test and will issue the case at standard rates for Rs. 4 lacs endowment policy that he has applied for.

Facts of the Case

- Santosh is slightly overweight on medical examination.
- Has a blood pressure which is slightly above normal range.
- The weight and blood pressure by itself are not in the ranges that would attract extra premium.

What should be Mr. Lekhak's decision? Should he call for a fasting blood sugar test? If the test result comes back as normal what should be his decision?

Case Solution

Mr. Lekhak decides to call for a fasting blood Sugar test.

The fasting blood report comes back as normal. Mr. Lekhak further reflects over the case. He finds that Santosh has the following three borderline risk factors:

- A family history of diabetes
- Slight overweight
- Slight high blood pressure

Taking all these factors into totality, Mr. Lekhak rates the case +25 even though none of the risk factors independently are ratable.

SOLUTION 5

UNDERWRITING HAZARDOUS OCCUPATION

Two army officers, Major Seva Singh and Captain Yudha Vir Singh apply for life insurance policies. The case files come to Dr. Nirikshak Sharma a supervisor in Bhavishya Life Insurance Company.

Facts of the Case

- Major Seva Singh is a permanent regular commissioned officer in the Army Service Corps. He is stationed at a large army base supply depot in Kolkata. He takes care of transportation, purchase and demands of supplies of the area under his jurisdiction. He has never been posted to forward areas so far but he may be posted to forward areas during in his service. Although he is eligible for posting to a field area but his role will be limited to non-combat duties viz. handling of purchase and distribution of army supplies.
- Captain Yudha Vir Singh is also in the Army. He is an infantry man. He is currently posted to Delhi in the army headquarters on staff duties. In his career, in the army, he has participated in many combat operations on the borders.

You are a junior underwriter under Nirikshak. He sends for you and hands over the two case files to you and asks you as to which of the two army officers will you charge extra premium for occupational risk? What will be your response?

Case Solution

Even if the guidelines book states that army personnel are high risk clients, in the case of Major Seva Singh the underwriter may decide to place him in the low risk category as he is in non-combat duties and not charge extra on life insurance cover. Captain Yudha Vir Singh, however is an infantry officer whose basic duties involve risky combats. Even if he is temporarily posted on a peace time staff job his job continues to carry an extra life risk. Therefore, he will be given a minimum of 2 per mille loading on life cover and will not be given any accident rider.

SOLUTION 6

RESIDENTIAL RISKS

Underwriter Miss Smart received a case of Mr Videshi working in Kenya for life insurance coverage. He has an administrative job in human resources department in a company registered and operating in Kenya. According to the underwriting manual Kenya is in the category of risk that has to be declined.

Miss Smart goes exactly by the book and declines the case. Is she right in her decision?

Case Solution

Miss Smart is right is her decision. The residential risk factors in the proposal (refer to chapter 3 for life insurance coverage risk for persons living in high risk areas) warrant a declinature.

SOLUTION 7

FOREIGN NATIONALS RESIDING IN INDIA

Mr Crown, a British man is a teacher of English in a public school in the famous Choli Ghaghra town in Rajasthan for the last 10 years. He is working on a research project tracing the history of the area. He is married to Dr. Bharti who teaches Principles and Practices of Life insurance in the University of Jaipur. He has no medical history or health problems. On Deepavali day both husband and wife meet Beema Kumar the local life insurance agent of Bhavishya Life Insurance Company.

You are an underwriter in Bhavishya Life Insurance Company. The following day Beema Kumar rings you up to confirm whether your company would give Mr Crown (who is not an Indian citizen) a life insurance policy. How would you answer the question?

Case Solution

As per guidelines followed by the life insurance companies in India there is no bar on giving life insurance policies to foreign nationals. Accordingly Mr. Crown will be given a life insurance policy on standard rates.

ANNEXURES

ANNEXURE 1

PREMIUM TABLES

(1) Reliance Term Insurance Plan

Term Assurance Rates — Reliance Term Plan — Male Lives

Note : Premium Rates per 1000 Sum Assured without policy fee.

Age/Term	*5*	*6*	*7*	*8*	*9*	*10*	*11*	*12*	*13*	*14*	*15*	*16*	*17*	*18*
(1)	*(2)*	*(3)*	*(4)*	*(5)*	*(6)*	*(7)*	*(8)*	*(9)*	*(10)*	*(11)*	*(12)*	*(13)*	*(14)*	*(15)*
21	1.60	1.60	1.60	1.60	1.60	1.60	1.60	1.60	1.60	1.60	1.60	1.60	1.60	1.60
22	1.63	1.63	1.63	1.63	1.63	1.63	1.63	1.63	1.63	1.63	1.63	1.63	1.63	1.63
23	1.65	1.65	1.65	1.65	1.65	1.65	1.65	1.65	1.65	1.65	1.65	1.65	1.65	1.65
24	1.66	1.66	1.66	1.66	1.66	1.66	1.66	1.66	1.66	1.66	1.66	1.66	1.66	1.66
25	1.68	1.68	1.68	1.68	1.68	1.68	1.68	1.68	1.68	1.68	1.68	1.68	1.68	1.68
26	1.69	1.69	1.69	1.69	1.69	1.69	1.69	1.69	1.69	1.69	1.69	1.69	1.69	1.69
27	1.69	1.69	1.69	1.69	1.69	1.69	1.69	1.69	1.69	1.69	1.69	1.69	1.69	1.69
28	1.70	1.70	1.70	1.70	1.70	1.70	1.70	1.70	1.70	1.70	1.70	1.70	1.71	1.75
29	1.71	1.71	1.71	1.71	1.71	1.71	1.71	1.71	1.71	1.71	1.71	1.75	1.79	1.84
30	1.73	1.73	1.73	1.73	1.73	1.73	1.73	1.73	1.73	1.75	1.79	1.84	1.89	1.95

(Contd.)

ANNEXURE 1 (Contd.)

Age/Term	5	6	7	8	9	10	11	12	13	14	15	16	17	18
(1)	(2)	(3)	(4)	(5)	(6)	(7)	(8)	(9)	(10)	(11)	(12)	(13)	(14)	(15)
31	1.77	1.77	1.77	1.77	1.77	1.77	1.77	1.77	1.80	1.84	1.89	1.95	2.01	2.09
32	1.82	1.82	1.82	1.82	1.82	1.82	1.82	1.86	1.90	1.95	2.01	2.08	2.16	2.24
33	1.89	1.89	1.89	1.89	1.89	1.89	1.93	1.97	2.02	2.09	2.16	2.24	2.33	2.42
34	1.98	1.98	1.98	1.98	1.98	2.01	2.05	2.11	2.17	2.24	2.33	2.42	2.52	2.63
35	2.08	2.08	2.08	2.08	2.10	2.14	2.19	2.26	2.34	2.42	2.52	2.62	2.74	2.86
36	2.20	2.20	2.20	2.21	2.24	2.29	2.36	2.44	2.53	2.63	2.74	2.86	2.99	3.12
37	2.34	2.34	2.34	2.36	2.41	2.47	2.55	2.64	2.74	2.86	2.99	3.12	3.26	3.42
38	2.50	2.50	2.50	2.53	2.59	2.67	2.76	2.87	2.99	3.12	3.27	3.41	3.57	3.74
39	2.67	2.67	2.68	2.73	2.80	2.90	3.01	3.13	3.27	3.42	3.57	3.74	3.92	4.11
40	2.85	2.85	2.89	2.95	3.04	3.15	3.28	3.43	3.58	3.74	3.92	4.11	4.30	4.50
41	3.05	3.06	3.12	3.20	3.31	3.44	3.59	3.75	3.93	4.11	4.31	4.51	4.72	4.93
42	3.27	3.30	3.37	3.48	3.61	3.77	3.93	4.12	4.31	4.52	4.73	4.95	5.17	5.39
43	3.52	3.58	3.67	3.81	3.96	4.13	4.32	4.53	4.75	4.97	5.20	5.43	5.66	5.90
44	3.83	3.90	4.02	4.18	4.35	4.55	4.77	4.99	5.22	5.47	5.71	5.95	6.20	6.47
45	4.18	4.28	4.42	4.59	4.80	5.02	5.25	5.50	5.75	6.00	6.25	6.52	6.80	7.09
46	4.59	4.71	4.87	5.07	5.30	5.54	5.79	6.05	6.31	6.58	6.86	7.15	7.46	7.78
47	5.04	5.18	5.37	5.60	5.84	6.10	6.38	6.64	6.92	7.21	7.52	7.84	8.18	8.54

48	5.55	5.70	5.93	6.17	6.44	6.72	7.00	7.28	7.58	7.90	8.24	8.60	8.97	—
49	6.10	6.29	6.53	6.79	7.08	7.36	7.66	7.97	8.30	8.65	9.03	9.43	—	—
50	6.70	6.92	7.18	7.46	7.75	8.05	8.38	8.72	9.09	9.48	9.90	—	—	—
51	7.35	7.60	7.87	8.16	8.47	8.80	9.15	9.54	9.95	10.39	—	—	—	—
52	8.06	8.32	8.60	8.90	9.24	9.60	10.01	10.44	10.90	—	—	—	—	—
53	8.82	9.07	9.36	9.70	10.07	10.49	10.94	11.43	—	—	—	—	—	—
54	9.59	9.86	10.18	10.57	11.00	11.47	11.98	—	—	—	—	—	—	—
55	10.40	10.70	11.08	11.52	12.01	12.55	—	—	—	—	—	—	—	—
56	11.27	11.63	12.08	12.59	13.14	—	—	—	—	—	—	—	—	—
57	12.23	12.67	13.19	13.77	—	—	—	—	—	—	—	—	—	—
58	13.32	13.84	14.44	—	—	—	—	—	—	—	—	—	—	—
59	14.60	15.20	—	—	—	—	—	—	—	—	—	—	—	—
60	16.08	—	—	—	—	—	—	—	—	—	—	—	—	—

Annexure 1 (*Contd.*)

(2) Reliance Endowment Plan

Table of Premium Rates (Regular)—Reliance Endowment Plan

Age/Term	*5*	*6*	*7*	*8*	*9*	*10*	*11*	*12*	*13*	*14*	*15*	*16*	*17*
(1)	*(2)*	*(3)*	*(4)*	*(5)*	*(6)*	*(7)*	*(8)*	*(9)*	*(10)*	*(11)*	*(12)*	*(13)*	*(14)*
20	223.12	182.37	153.89	132.87	116.72	103.92	93.52	84.92	77.68	71.50	67.53	62.74	58.53
21	223.13	182.38	153.90	132.88	116.73	103.93	93.53	84.93	77.69	71.51	67.55	62.76	58.55
22	223.14	182.39	153.91	132.89	116.74	103.93	93.54	84.94	77.70	71.53	67.56	62.77	58.57
23	223.15	182.39	153.92	132.90	116.74	103.94	93.55	84.95	77.71	71.54	67.58	62.79	58.60
24	223.15	182.40	153.92	132.90	116.75	103.95	93.56	84.96	77.73	71.56	67.60	62.82	58.63
25	223.15	182.40	153.93	132.91	116.76	103.96	93.58	84.98	77.75	71.59	67.63	62.85	58.66
26	223.16	182.40	153.93	132.92	116.77	103.98	93.60	85.00	77.78	71.62	67.67	62.89	58.71
27	223.16	182.41	153.95	132.93	116.79	104.00	93.62	85.04	77.81	71.66	67.71	62.94	58.76
28	223.18	182.43	153.97	132.96	116.82	104.04	93.66	85.08	77.86	71.71	67.77	63.00	58.82
29	223.20	182.46	154.00	133.00	116.86	104.08	93.71	85.13	77.92	71.77	67.84	63.08	58.90
30	223.24	182.50	154.04	133.04	116.91	104.14	93.77	85.20	77.98	71.84	67.92	63.16	59.00
31	223.28	182.55	154.10	133.10	116.98	104.20	93.84	85.27	78.06	71.93	68.01	63.26	59.10
32	223.33	182.61	154.16	133.17	117.05	104.28	93.92	85.36	78.16	72.02	68.12	63.38	59.22
33	223.39	182.67	154.23	133.25	117.13	104.37	94.02	85.45	78.26	72.13	68.24	63.51	59.36

34	223.47	182.75	154.32	133.33	117.22	104.47	94.12	85.56	78.38	72.26	68.38	63.65	59.52
35	223.55	182.84	154.41	133.43	117.33	104.58	94.24	85.69	78.51	72.40	68.54	63.82	59.69
36	223.64	182.94	154.51	133.54	117.44	104.70	94.37	85.83	78.66	72.56	68.71	64.00	59.89
37	223.75	183.05	154.63	133.66	117.57	104.84	94.51	85.99	78.83	72.74	68.91	64.21	60.11
38	223.85	183.16	154.75	133.79	117.71	104.99	94.68	86.16	79.01	72.93	69.12	64.44	60.35
39	223.96	183.28	154.88	133.94	117.87	105.16	94.86	86.35	79.22	73.15	69.36	64.69	60.62
40	224.09	183.42	155.03	134.11	118.05	105.35	95.06	86.57	79.45	73.40	69.63	64.98	60.91
41	224.25	183.59	155.22	134.30	118.26	105.57	95.30	86.82	79.72	73.68	69.94	65.30	61.25
42	224.43	183.79	155.43	134.53	118.50	105.83	95.57	87.11	80.02	74.00	70.28	65.65	61.62
43	224.64	184.02	155.67	134.78	118.77	106.11	95.87	87.43	80.35	74.34	70.65	66.04	62.02
44	224.88	184.27	155.94	135.07	119.07	106.43	96.21	87.78	80.71	74.72	71.06	66.47	62.47
45	225.15	184.56	156.24	135.39	119.41	106.78	96.57	88.16	81.11	75.13	71.51	66.93	62.96
46	225.44	184.87	156.57	135.74	119.77	107.16	96.97	88.57	81.54	75.58	71.99	67.44	63.49
47	225.76	185.21	156.93	136.11	120.16	107.57	97.39	89.01	82.00	76.07	72.52	67.99	64.07
48	226.11	185.58	157.32	136.52	120.59	108.01	97.85	89.49	82.50	76.59	73.09	68.59	64.70
49	226.49	185.98	157.74	136.96	121.04	108.48	98.34	90.01	83.05	77.17	73.72	69.25	65.38
50	226.90	186.41	158.18	137.42	121.52	108.99	98.87	90.57	83.64	77.79	74.39	69.96	66.14
51	227.33	186.86	158.65	137.91	122.04	109.53	99.45	91.18	84.28	78.47	75.13	70.74	66.96
52	227.78	187.33	159.15	138.43	122.59	110.12	100.08	91.84	84.98	79.21	75.95	71.60	67.88
53	228.25	187.82	159.68	138.99	123.19	110.77	100.76	92.56	85.75	80.02	76.85	72.56	68.89

(Contd.)

ANNEXURE 1 (Contd.)

Age/Term	5	6	7	8	9	10	11	12	13	14	15	16	17
(1)	(2)	(3)	(4)	(5)	(6)	(7)	(8)	(9)	(10)	(11)	(12)	(13)	(14)
54	228.74	188.35	160.25	139.61	123.86	111.48	101.51	93.36	86.60	80.93	77.85	73.63	70.03
55	229.26	188.93	160.88	140.30	124.60	112.26	102.35	94.25	87.55	81.94	78.98	74.83	71.30
56	229.90	189.63	161.63	141.11	125.45	113.16	103.31	95.28	88.64	83.11	80.27	76.20	72.76
57	230.65	190.44	162.51	142.02	126.41	114.19	104.40	96.45	89.90	84.45	81.74	77.76	74.41
58	231.52	191.37	163.47	143.04	127.50	115.35	105.65	97.78	91.32	85.96	83.41	79.53	76.27
59	232.49	192.38	164.54	144.18	128.72	116.66	107.06	99.28	92.92	87.66	85.29	81.51	—
60	233.52	193.47	165.72	145.45	130.10	118.14	108.64	100.97	94.72	89.58	87.40	—	—
61	234.62	194.68	167.04	146.88	131.64	119.80	110.42	102 87	96.74	91.72	—	—	—
62	235.83	196.02	168.51	148.49	133.38	121.67	112.42	105.01	99.01	—	—	—	—
63	237.16	197.53	170.17	150.30	135.34	123.78	114.68	107.42	—	—	—	—	—
64	239.05	199.55	172.34	152.61	137.79	126.38	117.43	—	—	—	—	—	—
65	241.15	201.81	174.75	155.18	140.53	129.28	—	—	—	—	—	—	—

ANNEXURE 1 (*Contd.*)

(3) Reliance Whole Life Plan

Table of Premium Rates—Reliance Whole Life Plan

Age/Term	*5*	*6*	*7*	*8*	*9*	*10*	*11*	*12*	*13*	*14*	*15*	*16*	*17*	*18*	*19*
(1)	*(2)*	*(3)*	*(4)*	*(5)*	*(6)*	*(7)*	*(8)*	*(9)*	*(10)*	*(11)*	*(12)*	*(13)*	*(14)*	*(15)*	*(16)*
20	81.15	68.10	59.15	52.65	47.70	43.80	40.65	38.10	35.95	34.15	32.60	31.25	30.10	29.05	28.15
21	82.85	69.50	60.40	53.70	48.65	44.70	41.50	38.90	36.70	34.85	33.30	31.90	30.70	29.65	28.75
22	84.55	70.95	61.65	54.85	49.65	45.65	42.35	39.70	37.45	35.60	33.95	32.60	31.35	30.30	29.35
23	86.35	72.45	62.90	56.00	50.70	46.60	43.25	40.55	38.25	36.35	34.70	33.25	32.00	30.95	29.95
24	88.15	74.00	64.25	57.15	51.80	47.55	44.20	41.40	39.10	37.10	35.40	33.95	32.70	31.60	30.60
25	90.05	75.60	65.65	58.40	52.90	48.60	45.15	42.30	39.90	37.90	36.20	34.70	33.40	32.30	31.25
26	92.00	77.20	67.05	59.65	54.05	49.65	46.10	43.20	40.80	38.75	37.00	35.45	34.15	33.00	31.95
27	94.00	78.90	68.55	61.00	55.25	50.75	47.15	44.15	41.70	39.60	37.80	36.25	34.90	33.75	32.70
28	96.10	80.65	70.05	62.30	56.45	51.85	48.20	45.15	42.60	40.50	38.65	37.10	35.70	34.50	33.40
29	98.25	82.45	71.60	63.75	57.75	53.05	49.30	46.15	43.60	41.40	39.55	37.95	36.55	35.30	34.20
30	100.45	84.30	73.20	65.15	59.05	54.25	50.40	47.25	44.60	42.35	40.45	38.80	37.35	36.10	35.00
31	102.75	86.20	74.90	66.65	60.40	55.50	51.55	48.30	45.60	43.35	41.40	39.70	38.25	36.95	35.85

(*Contd.*)

ANNEXURE 1 (Contd.)

Age/Term	5	6	7	8	9	10	11	12	13	14	15	16	17	18	19
(1)	(2)	(3)	(4)	(5)	(6)	(7)	(8)	(9)	(10)	(11)	(12)	(13)	(14)	(15)	(16)
32	105.05	88.20	76.60	68.20	61.80	56.75	52.75	49.45	46.70	44.35	42.35	40.65	39.15	37.85	36.70
33	107.45	90.20	78.35	69.75	63.20	58.10	53.95	50.60	47.80	45.40	43.35	41.60	40.10	38.75	37.55
34	109.95	92.30	80.20	71.35	64.70	59.45	55.25	51.80	48.90	46.50	44.40	42.60	41.05	39.70	38.50
35	112.45	94.40	82.05	73.05	66.20	60.85	56.55	53.00	50.10	47.60	45.50	43.65	42.05	40.65	39.45
36	115.05	96.60	83.95	74.70	67.75	62.25	57.90	54.25	51.25	48.75	46.55	44.70	43.10	41.65	40.40
37	117.70	98.85	85.90	76.45	69.30	63.75	59.25	55.55	52.50	49.90	47.70	45.80	44.15	42.70	41.45
38	120.40	101.10	87.90	78.25	70.95	65.25	60.65	56.90	53.75	51.15	48.90	46.95	45.25	43.80	42.50
39	123.15	103.45	89.90	80.10	72.60	66.80	62.10	58.25	55.05	52.40	50.10	48.10	46.40	44.90	43.55
40	126.00	105.85	92.00	81.95	74.35	68.35	63.60	59.65	56.40	53.65	51.30	49.30	47.55	46.05	44.70
41	129.15	108.50	94.35	84.05	76.25	70.15	65.25	61.25	57.90	55.10	52.70	50.65	48.85	47.30	45.95
42	132.35	111.25	96.75	86.20	78.25	72.00	66.95	62.90	59.50	56.60	54.15	52.05	50.25	48.65	47.25
43	135.70	114.05	99.20	88.45	80.25	73.90	68.75	64.55	61.10	58.15	55.65	53.50	51.65	50.05	48.60
44	139.10	116.95	101.75	90.70	82.35	75.80	70.60	66.30	62.75	59.75	57.20	55.00	53.10	51.45	50.00
45	142.60	119.90	104.35	93.05	84.50	77.85	72.45	68.10	64.45	61.40	58.80	56.55	54.65	52.95	51.50
46	146.15	122.95	107.00	95.45	86.70	79.90	74.40	69.95	66.20	63.10	60.45	58.15	56.20	54.50	53.00
47	149.75	126.00	109.75	97.95	89.00	82.00	76.40	71.85	68.05	64.85	62.15	59.85	57.80	56.10	54.60
48	153.45	129.15	112.50	100.45	91.30	84.15	78.45	73.75	69.90	66.65	63.90	61.55	59.50	57.75	56.20

49	157.25	132.40	115.35	103.00	93.65	86.35	80.55	75.75	71.80	68.50	65.70	63.30	61.25	59.50	57.95
50	161.10	135.70	118.30	105.65	96.10	88.65	82.70	77.85	73.80	70.45	67.60	65.15	63.10	61.30	59.75
51	165.05	139.05	121.25	108.35	98.60	91.00	84.90	79.95	75.90	72.45	69.55	67.10	65.00	63.20	61.60
52	169.00	142.45	124.30	111.10	101.15	93.40	87.20	82.15	78.00	74.55	71.60	69.10	67.00	65.15	—
53	173.10	145.95	127.40	113.95	103.80	95.85	89.55	84.45	80.20	76.70	73.70	71.20	69.05	—	—
54	177.20	149.50	130.55	116.85	106.50	98.45	92.05	86.80	82.55	78.95	75.95	73.45	—	—	—
55	181.45	153.20	133.85	119.85	109.30	101.10	94.60	89.30	84.95	81.35	78.35	—	—	—	—
56	185.85	157.00	137.30	123.00	112.25	103.95	97.30	91.90	87.55	83.90	—	—	—	—	—
57	190.40	160.95	140.85	126.30	115.35	106.90	100.15	94.70	90.30	—	—	—	—	—	—
58	195.15	165.10	144.60	129.75	118.60	110.00	103.20	97.70	—	—	—	—	—	—	—
59	200.05	169.40	148.45	133.35	122.05	113.30	106.40	—	—	—	—	—	—	—	—
60	205.00	173.75	152.45	137.10	125.60	116.75	—	—	—	—	—	—	—	—	—

Source of above tables: www.reliancelife.co.in

ANNEXURE 2

Published Mortality Table (Effective 01-01-2005)

Indian Assured Lives Mortality (1994-96) (modified) Ult.

Age *(x)*	*Mortality rate* (q_x)	*Age* *(x)*	*Mortality rate* (q_x)
(1)	*(2)*	*(3)*	*(4)*
0	0.001630	51	0.005819
1	0.000960	52	0.006443
2	0.000670	53	0.007116
3	0.000620	54	0.007839
4	0.000470	55	0.008611
5	0.000420	56	0.009433
6	0.000380	57	0.010294
7	0.000400	58	0.011025
8	0.000400	59	0.011951
9	0.000400	60	0.013073
10	0.000380	61	0.014391
11	0.000450	62	0.015904
12	0.000530	63	0.017612
13	0.000650	64	0.019516
14	0.000713	65	0.021615
15	0.000770	66	0.022724
16	0.000823	67	0.025617
17	0.000873	68	0.028823
18	0.000919	69	0.032372
19	0.000961	70	0.036294
20	0.000999	71	0.040623
21	0.001033	72	0.045392
22	0.001063	73	0.050639
23	0.001090	74	0.056404

(*Contd.*)

ANNEXURE 2 (*Contd.*)

(1)	*(2)*	*(3)*	*(4)*
24	0.001113	75	0.062728
25	0.001132	76	0.069655
26	0.001147	77	0.077231
27	0.001159	78	0.085502
28	0.001166	79	0.094519
29	0.001170	80	0.104331
30	0.001170	81	0.114992
31	0.001171	82	0.126553
32	0.001201	83	0.139067
33	0.001246	84	0.151077
34	0.001308	85	0.162298
35	0.001387	86	0.174149
36	0.001482	87	0.186638
37	0.001593	88	0.199775
38	0.001721	89	0.213560
39	0.001865	90	0.227995
40	0.002053	91	0.243072
41	0.002247	92	0.258782
42	0.002418	93	0.275109
43	0.002602	94	0.292031
44	0.002832	95	0.309522
45	0.003110	96	0.327549
46	0.003438	97	0.346073
47	0.003816	98	0.365052
48	0.004243	99	0.384436
49	0.004719	—	—
50	0.005244	—	—

Source : Actuarial society of India (website).
x = Age nearest birthday.
(q_x) = Probability of dying between age x to x+1.

In actuarial science, a life table (also called a mortality table or actuarial table) is a table which shows, persons at each age, what the probability is that they die before their next birthday. The mortality rates chart illustrates the increase in mortality as a person grows older. A Mortality Table shows the number of deaths per 1000 of a group of people. This chart is based on actual data of people insured by Life Insurance Corporation (LIC). Insurance companies charge premiums according to the mortality rate given in such tables. If the mortality rate increases so does the premium. This is an Ultimate Table (Ult.) which means that it excludes the first 5 to 10 years of experience of those who purchase life insurance. Experience shows that people have a lower mortality rate in the first years after they have purchased insurance, probably because they have recently passed medical and other tests. (A Select Mortality Table includes data only on people who have recently purchased insurance. An *aggregate mortality table* includes all data.)

ANNEXURE 3(A)

Sum and Age-linked Medical Requirements Table

Sum Assured (Rs.)	*Age Below 30 years*	*31 to 35 years*	*36 to 45 years*	*46 to 55 years*	*56 years and above*
(1)	*(2)*	*(3)*	*(4)*	*(5)*	*6)*
Below 10 Lacs	No Medical	No Medical	No Medical	No Medical	MER and ECG
10 to 20 Lacs	No Medical	No Medical	MER and ECG	MER and ECG	MER and ECG
20 to 40 Lacs	No Medical	MER and ECG	MER, ECG and Blood Chemistry	MER, ECG and Blood Chemistry	MER, Treadmill and Blood Chemistry
Above 40 Lacs	MER and ECG, HIV	MER, ECG and Blood Chemistry, HIV	MER, Treadmill and Blood Chemistry, HIV	MER, Treadmill and Blood Chemistry, HIV	MER, Treadmill and Blood Chemistry, HIV

Abbreviations

MER = Medical Examination Report
ECG = Electro cardiograph
HIV = Test to detect HIV AIDS
Treadmill = Exercise ECG

ANNEXURE 3(B)

Financial Requirements Table

Sum Assured below Rs. 10 lacs: No need for financial documents

Between Rs. 10 to 20 lacs: Financial forms or questionnaires or in some cases income tax returns.

Above Rs. 20 lacs: ITR for past 3 years/Chartered Accountant certified profit-loss statement and balance sheets.

ITR = Income Tax Returns

ANNEXURE 4

SAMPLE LIFE INSURANCE APPLICATION FORM

XYZ INSURANCE COMPANY LIMITED
Regd. Office—Address
Form No. XXXXXXX

Proposal where the Proposer is the Life to be Insured

Proposal for : Base Policy: [______________]

Riders: [______________________]

Type of Plan ____

Non-medical/Medical (select as appropriate)

Agent Name____________________ Agent number____________

Branch ____

Agent's contact phone no.________________________________

Declaration and Undertaking

You are required to disclose ALL material facts and circumstances to XYZ LIFE INSURANCE COMPANY LIMITED (hereinafter referred to as the "Company") in this proposal (the "Proposal"), which shall form the basis of the contract, otherwise the policy issued shall be voidable at the option of the Company. If you are in doubt as to whether any facts or circumstances are material or not, you must disclose them. (2) If any questions are not relevant, please state "N.A". Any correction or over writing in this Proposal must be initialled by you. (3) Please print or type in BLOCK LETTERS. (4) The initial payment must accompany this Proposal and may be paid by cash, crossed cheque, money order or bank draft made payable to XYZ INSURANCE COMPANY LIMITED, at the location of the Branch Office, or in any other manner as may be approved by the Company. It is clarified that cash payments must be made at any of the Company's Branch Offices only. (5) Receipt by the Company of the completed Proposal and the initial payment does not create any obligation on the part of the

Company to underwrite the risk, and the Company shall not be liable until such time it has underwritten the risk.

Statutory Warning as per Section 41 of Insurance Act, 1938 and Regulation 13 of the IRDA (Insurance Advertisements and Disclosure) Regulations, 2000.

No person shall allow or offer to allow, either directly or indirectly, as an inducement to any person to take out or renew or continue an insurance in respect of any kind of risk relating to lives or property in India, any rebate of the whole or part of the commission payable or any rebate of the premium shown on the policy, nor shall any person taking out or renewing or continuing a policy accept any rebate, except such rebate as may be allowed in accordance with the published prospectus or tables of the insurer. Any violation of this provision shall be an offence under Section 41 of the Insurance Act, 1938.

PART I
PERSONAL AND COVERAGE INFORMATION

1. Personal Details of Applicant

a. Title (Mr./Mrs./Ms./Any other ____________

b. Surname__________First Name________ Middle Name (s) ________

c. Father's/Husband's Name in full____________

d. Identification source and ID (Please mention accordingly) : PAN/ Passport/Driving License/Ration Card/Election Commission of India Voter Identity Card/other approved identification. Copy to be Provided and Original Shown ____________

e. Date of Birth ______dd_____mm______yyyy
Proof of Date of Birth (Copy to be provided and original shown)
____

f. Gender : Male ☐ Female ☐

f. Marital status : Single ☐ Married ☐

g. Income (Rs. per annum) ____________

h. Current Residential address ____________
____________PIN________
Phone No. (with STD code)_________Email Address: ________

i. Permanent Residential address ____________
____________PIN________
Phone No. (with STD code) ____________

j. Preferred Language____________

Work Details

k. Work status (salaried/self-employed/unemployed, etc.) ________

l. Present occupation ____________

m. (IF EMPLOYED) Please state your designation and provide a brief job description :

n. Job Description ____________

o. Employer's name ____________

o. Industry/Nature of business ____________

p. Workplace address ____________
____________PIN________
Phone No. (with STD code)____________Extn. ________
Mobile No. ____________

q. Self-employed? Yes ☐ No. ☐
Please provide details of the nature of work ____________

r. Any previous employment or occupation within the previous 2 years
____

s. Preferred mailing address Work ☐ Current Residence ☐ Permanent ☐

2. Coverage Information

Non-forfeiture Options (please select one)

Extended Term Insurance ☐
Reduced paid up Insurance

Premium Mode (please select one

Annual	Semi-annual	Quarterly	Monthly
☐	☐	☐	☐

Modal Premium (to be filled in by the agent)

Base Plan	*Coverage Amount (in Rs.)*	*Modal Premium (in Rs.)*
Riders		

Total Modal Premium (in Rs.)________________]
Paid Rs ________________ Cash/Crossed Cheque/Money Order/Bank Draft/ Credit card/Direct Debit Details ____________________________________
(Please give cheque /m.o./bank draft/credit card no. & bank details).
Future Payment Mode : Cash/Crossed Cheque/Money Order/Bank Draft/ Credit card/Direct Debit.
Any cheque, draft, or other payment instrument given for the payment must be honoured on first presentation for payment.
Desired Date of Policy _____/_____/________ It is clarified that any payment made (other than by way of cash) shall be considered as received by the Company only after the amount has been credited to the account of the Company on first presentation.

3. Nomination

Complete name	*Address of the nominee*	*Relationship to the Life Insured*	*Identification source (like Passport, PAN etc. Copy to be provided and original shown)*	*Proportion of Sum Insured/ benefits*

If the nominee is a minor, please name a person (the "Appointee") to receive the policy proceeds in the event of death of the Proposer while the nominee is still a minor, and provide below the address and relationship of such Appointee with the nominee.

Name of the Appointee ______________________

Address ______________________

Phone No. ______________________

Relationship to Nominee ______________________

4. MISCELLANEOUS

a. Do you currently have, or had in the last three years, any life, accident, disability, critical illness or medical insurance or any other insurance policy (with this or any other insurer)? If yes, please provide following details:

Name of Insurer	*Type and term of the Policy*	*Sum assured (including all benefits)*	*Date of issue*

b. (i) Have you made any claims under any such policy or scheme within the last 3 years? If so, please give full particulars of illnesses which gave rise to this claim and of the expenses incurred that were the subject of such claims.

(ii) Were any claims wholly or partially rejected ? If so, please give full particulars.

c. Has any proposal or application for reinstatement made by you (to this or any other insurer) been ever (i) refused, withdrawn, or otherwise not accepted; (ii) Accepted but with extra premium or lien; (iii) Accepted on terms other than those proposed by you? If yes, please tick the relevant box below with a ______ and give details as required below:

Details of Proposal	*Name of the insurer*	*Details*

PART II

PERSONAL MEDICAL DETAILS OF THE PROPOSED LIFE INSURED

1. Family History:

	If living		*If deceased*	
	Age at last birthday	*Give details on the state of health and full particulars of any major illnesses:*	*Age at death*	*death death*
Father				
Mother				
Brothers				
Sisters				

Details of Health of Spouse ____________________

2. State the name and address of your doctor____________________

Dr. Address:

Phone No:

Registration No:

3. (a) Height _____m_____cm OR _______ft______inch
   (b) Weight (in kgs) ________kg
   (c) Have you had a recent noticeable gain or loss of weight. If "Yes", provide details:
4. Are you now suffering from or have you ever suffered from any of the following conditions? If yes, please provide details.

	Yes	No.
(a) Chest pain, palpitation, rheumatic fever, heart murmur, heart attack, shortness of breath or other heart disorder, Stroke or elevated blood pressure?	☐	☐
(b) Diabetes;	☐	☐
(c) Glandular or thyroid disorder?	☐	☐
(d) Respiratory disorder, shortness of breath, bronchitis, asthma, tuberculosis, persistent cough or any other respiratory disorder?	☐	☐
(e) Congenital disorder, anaemia, leukemia or disorder of the blood?	☐	☐
(f) Cancer, tumour, cyst, lump or disorder of skin or lymph gland or other malignancy?	☐	☐
(g) Abnormalities in urine, stone or other disorder of kidney, prostrate or bladder ?	☐	☐

(h) Any ulcer, colitis, gallstones, indigestion or other disorder of stomach, gall bladder or intestinal disorder? ☐ ☐
(i) Any liver disorders like jaundice, hepatitis, cirrhosis, etc.?
(j) Any episodes of epilepsy or nervous disorder, multiple sclerosis, tremors, numbness, double vision or giddiness, speech defect, paralysis? ☐ ☐
(k) Any episodes of psychiatric disorders, depression? ☐ ☐
(l) Any form of eye, ear, nose, or throat disorder? ☐ ☐
(m) Any gynaecological disorder? ☐ ☐
(n) Any disorder of back, muscle, joints, bone, neck or deformity, amputation, gout or arthritis?

5. Smoking and drinking—
   (5.1) Do you or have you ever taken alcohol, narcotics or psychotropic substance? If "Yes", please state quantity and type of alcohol, narcotics or psychotropic substance per week. ________________
   (5.2) Have you smoked cigarettes or ever consumed tobacco in any other form in the last 12 months? If "Yes", please indicate the average number of cigarettes smoked and/or average quantity of tobacco consumed per day ______________
6. Please answer the following questions, and if your answer to any of the questions is in the affirmative, please provide relevant details
   (a) In the last 5 years, have you ever had, or been advised to have, or are you likely within the next 30 days to have an X-ray, CT scaning, MRI, Ultrasonography, ECG, blood test or any other investigatory or diagnostic tests? Yes No.
   (b) Have you ever undergone any type of surgery or surgical treatment in the last five years? ☐ ☐
   (c) Have you ever been tested positive for HIV/AIDS or Hepatitis B or C OR have you been tested/treated for sexually transmitted disease(STD)? ☐ ☐
   (d) Have you ever suffered or are suffering from any other illness, condition other than that mentioned above or are undergoing any kind of investigation or treatment for the same ? ☐ ☐
7. This question is applicable only to females. If the answer to any of the questions is in the affirmative, please provide relevant details—
   (a) In the last 10 years, have you consulted a physician or medical practitioner for, or been treated for, or been informed that you have or have had a disorder of the pelvic organs or breast, or relating to menses or pregnancy?.
   (b) Are you pregnant now? If " Yes", how many months?
   (c) Have you ever had any abortion, miscarriage or caesarean section?

PART III

OTHER DETAILS

1. Hazardous Activities:

1.1 Do you take part or do you have any intention of taking part in any of the following activities :
parachuting,
hang gliding,
diving,
mountaineering,
flying (other than as bonafide passenger)

1.2 Please specify with full particulars any other activities in which you take part or intend in the next 30 days, to take part that is or is likely to be hazardous to health or personal safety.

2 **Any other information/Special remarks:**

DECLARATION AND CONFIRMATION BY THE PROPOSER

I hereby declare that:

I fully understand the meaning and scope of the questions contained above and am submitting the completed Proposal on my own volition, and I confirm that I have not been induced by anyone to make the Proposal.

The statements and declarations herein shall be the basis of a contract between me and the Company and if any untrue statement be contained herein, the Company shall have the right to cancel the Policy and forfeit any payments received.

have made complete, true and accurate disclosure of all the facts and circumstances as may be relevant, and have not withheld any information that maybe relevant to enable the Company to make an informed decision about the acceptability of the Proposal. The Company shall not be bound by any statement that is not made in the Proposal unless such statements are made in writing and received by the Company before the Company has underwritten the risk. Should any statements be incomplete, wrong or inaccurate, or should there be any omissions on my part in disclosing the relevant information, the Company shall have the right to cancel the Policy and forfeit any payments received

Should there be any change in any of the statements made in the Proposal from the time of my submission of the Proposal to the Company till the time the Company has underwritten the risk and issued the Policy, I shall forthwith inform the Company in writing, failing which the Company may cancel the Policy and forfeit the payments received.

I confirm that any information provided in relation to the Proposal may be used by the Company in any manner including for purposes of verification of such information. The Company may also share such information with any other persons including its affiliates and reinsurers. Notwithstanding any law, usage, custom, privilege or other rights available to me, the Company may make any independent verification of the facts as may be considered relevant by the Company from any source whatsoever. The Company may charge a fee in relation to any extraordinary costs as may be incurred by the Company in relation to processing of the Proposal and other matters referred to in the Proposal.

I UNDERSTAND AND AGREE THAT, I have the right to cancel this Proposal and/or the Policy by written request to the Company within 10 (ten) days from the receipt of the Policy, in which case the premium paid less any medical fees and administrative expenses incurred by the Company will be refunded to me without interest. If the Policy is sent by post it shall be deemed to have been delivered and received in the ordinary course of the post within three (3) days of posting.

[Signature of the Proposer]
[Name of the Proposer]
[Date]
[Place]
[Signature, name and address of the witness]

In case the Proposer is illiterate his/her left thumb impression should be attested by a person of standing unconnected with the Company but whose identity can easily be established and this declaration should be made by him.

Declaration by the person filling the form
Declarant's name & address

____

____

Pin

I hereby declare that I have fully explained the contents of this Proposal to the Proposer in the language understood by the Proposer and that the Proposer has affixed his/her left thumb impression to this Proposal after fully understanding the contents thereof.

Signature

Declaration to be made by a person of standing unconnected with the Company but whose identity can be easily established to the effect that the statements and declarations made hereinabove have been explained to the Proposer in vernacular language and he/she has appended his/her signature after fully understanding the same.

Declaration by the person filling the form
Declarant's name & address:

____

____

Pin

I hereby declare that I have fully explained the above questions to the Proposer and I have truthfully recorded the answers given by the Proposer.

Signature

ANNEXURE 5

SAMPLE MEDICAL EXAMINATION REPORT FORM

	Proposal Number (Copied from medical check-up form)	Agent's name: Agent code:

MEDICAL EXAMINATION REPORT

1. a. Full name of the person being examined: ______________________
   b. Date of birth: _____dd_____mm_____yy. c. Sex: ______
   d. Passport/PAN/License no. ______________________

PART I : (Questions to be put by the medical examiner)

2. a. Family History	Age if living	Health condition	Age at death	Year	Cause of death
Father	_______	_______	_______	_______	_______
Mother	_______	_______	_______	_______	_______
Brother(s)	_______	_______	_______	_______	_______
Sister(s)	_______	_______	_______	_______	_______

2. b. Is there any family history of diabetes, stroke, high blood pressure or nervous disorder, or are there any other hereditary disorders? If so please give details in column no. 12.

3. a. Name and address of your personal physician (if none, or if not consulted in last five years, so state.) b. Date of last consultation, reason and result:

Give the following information, so far as known for the person being examined. If "Yes", to any question, give full details in column no. 12:

4. Have you EVER had or been treated or been told you had:	**YES**	**NO**
a. Chest pain, breathlessness, palpitation, other heart diseases, anemia or other blood disorders?	☐	☐
b. Diabetes, thyroid or other endocrine disorder?	☐	☐
c. Chronic bronchitis, emphysema or other lung and respiratory tract disorder?	☐	☐
d. Cancer, tumor, cyst or any abnormal growth?	☐	☐
e. Recurrent indigestion, ulcer, colitis, jaundice, hepatitis or other diseases of liver, gall bladder, pancreas, stomach, intestine, rectum or anus?	☐	☐
f. AIDS, AIDS-related complex(ARC) or other immune deficiency?	☐	☐
g. Collagen diseases such as rheumatoid arthritis or lupus, etc.?	☐	☐
h. Elevated blood pressure, stroke or other circulatory disorder?	☐	☐
i. Sugar, blood or albumin in urine, venereal disease or disorder of kidney, prostate, urinary or genital system?	☐	☐

j. Seizures, dizziness or fainting; other nervous system disorder? ☐ ☐
k. Congenital disorder? ☐ ☐
l. Psychiatric, emotional or mental disorder, disorder from the use of alcohol or drugs? ☐ ☐
m. Back, spine, joints, muscular or bone disorder? ☐ ☐
n. Eye, ear, nose, throat or skin disorder? ☐ ☐

5. Have you ever smoked cigarettes in last 12 Months? If "Yes", please state number of cigarettes per day ☐ ☐
6. Do you or have you ever taken alcohol, narcotics or drugs? If "Yes" please give details: ☐ ☐
7. Are you currently taking medication? ☐ ☐
8. In the last two years, have you ever had unexplained weight loss or swollen glands, recurring diarrhea, fever or infection, persistent cough, pneumonia or thrush? ☐ ☐
9. In the past five years have you had:
   a. X-ray, CT scanning, MRI, Ultrasonography, ECG, Blood or Urine tests or other diagnostic tests such as ELISA, Australian antigen test, etc. ☐ ☐
   b. Illness, injury, surgery, medical advice, Hospital treatment or check up not mentioned above? ☐ ☐
10. **FOR FEMALES ONLY:**
    Disease of the breast or genital organs, complication of pregnancy, menstrual disorders, abnormal mammogram, pap smear, ultrasound of breast or pelvis or cone biopsy ? ☐ ☐

    Are you now pregnant, ☐ ☐
    If Yes, state number of months pregnant.

11. Give full details for each "Yes" answer in question numbers 4-10:

a. Question No.	b. Reason—Nature and severity of condition (Include frequency, diagnosis, treatment, medication, surgery and results)	c. Onset mm/yyyy	d. Recovery mm/yyyy	e. Names and addresses of physicians, hospital or medical facilities
______	______________	______	______	______
______	______________	______	______	______
______	______________	______	______	______
______	______________	______	______	______
______	______________	______	______	______
______	______________	______	______	______
______	______________	______	______	______
______	______________	______	______	______

DECLARATION:
I hereby declare that to the best of my knowledge and belief all the answers given above are true and complete, and that they shall be held to form part of the application now being made on my life with

Witness to signature **Signature of life examined** **Date:**
Medical officer examining

________________ ________________ ________

PART II (Questions to be answered by the medical examiner)

1. Are you related to the Person Examined (If Yes, please specify)
   Yes No ____________________
2. Has the Person examined ever consulted you for any other reason than insurance examination Yes No ____________
3. Appearance:
   a. What is the general appearance and configuration of the applicant? ____________
   b. Does the appearance correspond with the age stated? ____________
   c. Are there any personal peculiarities, defects or scars? ____________
4. Measurements:
   a. Height (without shoes) ___ft___ ins or ___ cms
   b. Weight (in indoor clothes) by actual weighing ____kg
   c. Chest circumference full inspiration___ins ___m___
      full expiration ___ins ___m___
   d. Abdominal circumference over umbilicus___ins ___m___
   e. Has there been any recent gain or loss in weight?
      If so please comment: ____________
5. Cardiovascular Examination
   a. Is there any evidence of cardiac hypertrophy, failure or other cardiovascular abnormalities excluding murmur? Yes No
   b. Is murmur present? (if yes give details) Yes No
      ____
   c. Situation of apex beat ____________________
   d. Is the heart enlarged? Yes ☐ No ☐ If yes, slight? ____moderate? _____marked? ____________
   e. Pulse (If over 90 please recount at end of examination) Rate______ Quality _______ Rhythm_______
   f. State of blood vessels________________
   g. The present condition of any varicose veins (state if support is or should be worn) ____________
   h. Blood-pressure (Readings to nearest 5 mm Hg) (If the first reading exceeds 140/90, 2 further readings should be taken after a five minute interval, diastolic to be at fifth phase i.e. cessation of sound
      1. Systolic______ Diastolic_______, 2. Systolic______ Diastolic_______
      3. Systolic______ Diastolic_______

i. If there is a history of diabetes, hypertension or cardiovascular disease Please comment on ankle pulse__________retinoscopy__________________

For each YES answer in questions 6 through 9, give full details in question 10

6. Is there evidence of past or present disease or disorder of:

	YES	NO
a. Brain or Nervous System? (please test major reflexes)		
b. Lungs or other parts of respiratory system?	☐	☐
c. Abdomen including gastrointestinal tract and Hernia?	☐	☐
d. Ears, Eyes, Nose, throat, Neck, Lymph nodes or other abnormal swellings?	☐	☐
e. Bones, Joints, Arteries, Veins or Skin?	☐	☐
f. Urinary and generative organs	☐	☐
g. Any other part of body excluding CVS.	☐	☐

7. Is there any paralysis, deformity, lameness or loss of limb?
8. Urinalysis (Do not complete if person examined is less than 12 years old)
   Albumin_______ Sugar _______ Occult Blood________Deposits_________
   Reaction________ Specific Gravity________
9. Please give question number and details to all YES answers
   Question Number Explanation

   __________ ____
   __________ ____
   __________ ____
   __________ ____
   __________ ____

PART III

In your opinion, is there anything about the examined person's health, lifestyle, character or mode of life which might unfavorably affect insurability?

Are there any points upon which you consider it desirable to obtain further information from the Medical attendant or other doctor who has been consulted? Special points (please add any other remarks which, in your opinion, may be of assistance in the final assessment of the risk)

____
____
____
____

I certify that I have carefully examined the person in private and I have asked each question exactly as set forth on the reverse side of this sheet and that the answers thereto are exactly as made to me, and that they have been signed in my presence. I believe all answers to be correctly recorded, complete and true. I hereby certify that the applicant's identification document and number is true and valid to the best of my knowledge.

Medical examiner's name, qualifications and rubber-stamp
signature:__________________
(Block capitals) ___________________

____

Medical examiner's

Date: ____________________

Address ___________________

____

ANNEXURE 6

RATING FOR NON-MEDICAL RISK FACTORS

Flat extra

There is a scientific reason behind method of charging extra premium or rating the case. This method depends on the type of risk that the extra premium is being charged for. The 'flat extra' and the 'multiplier' are two methods used for charging extra premium due to non-medical factors. Flat extra is generally imposed on cases where the extra risk is due to occupation or residential factors and would remain constant the whole time a client is in the particular job or area. The medical risks which generally increase with age are rated up by a different method through Extra Mortality Rating. Under the flat extra method the standard premium for the policy is increased by a specified number of rupees per 1000 of the sum assured for life insurance. This does not vary with age of the applicant or the type of plan. The underwriter may specify that the 'flat extra' be paid through out the term of the plan or only for a short duration till the risk exists. The flat extra premium method is normally used when the hazard is thought to be constant. (Residence risks: Is generally constant (e.g.) risk of staying in Congo will remain constant for the entire time a person resides there). The flat extra method is widely used to cover risks associated with certain occupations and avocations. Multiplier method is used to rate up accident riders for occupation and avocation causes and is simply the multiple of the premium

Flat extra example

If a client has a risky occupation and has applied for a policy of Rs. 1 lac. The premium he is paying is Rs. 2000.

The underwriter rates him 2 per Mil (also written as 2 pm)

Rs. 2 per 1000 so for 100,000 = Rs. 200 extra premium

200 added to original standard premium 2000 = 2200 rated premium.

Multiplier example

2x = 2 multiplied by the premium

If the accident rider premium is 150 and the underwriter wants to rate up 3x

Then $150 \times 3 = 450$ will be the premium the client has to pay for the rider.

ANNEXURE 7

INSURANCE REGULATORY AND DEVELOPMENT AUTHORITY (PROTECTION OF POLICYHOLDERS' INTERESTS) REGULATIONS, 2002

In exercise of the powers conferred by clause (zc) of sub-section (2) of section 114A of the Insurance Act, 1938 (4 of 1938) read with sections 14 and 26 of the Insurance Regulatory and Development Authority Act, 1999 (41 of 1999), the Authority, in consultation with the Insurance Advisory Committee, hereby makes the following regulations, namely:

Short Title and Commencement

1\. (1) These regulations may be called the Insurance Regulatory and Development Authority (Protection of Policyholders' Interests) Regulations, 2002.

(2) They shall come into force on the date of their publication in the Official Gazette and shall apply to all contracts of insurance effected thereafter, except regulation 4(1) which shall come into force on 1st October, 2002.

(3) These Regulations are in addition to any other regulations made by the Authority, which may, *inter alia,* provide for protection of the interest of policyholders.

(4) These Regulations apply to all insurers, insurance agents, insurance intermediaries and policyholders.

Definitions

2\. (1) In these regulations, unless the context otherwise requires:

(a) "Act" means the Insurance Act, 1938 (4 of 1938);

(b) "Authority" means the Insurance Regulatory and Development Authority established under the provisions of section 3 of the Insurance Regulatory and Development Authority Act, 1999 (41 of 1999);

(c) "Cover" means an insurance contract whether in the form of a policy or a cover note or a Certificate of Insurance or any other form prevalent in the industry to evidence the existence of an insurance contract;

(d) "Proposal form" means a form to be filled in by the proposer for insurance, for furnishing all material information required by the insurer in respect of a risk, in order to enable the insurer to decide whether to accept or decline, to undertake the risk, and in the event of acceptance of the risk, to determine the rates, terms and conditions of a cover to be granted.

Explanation: "Material" for the purpose of these regulations shall mean and include all important, essential and relevant information in the context of underwriting the risk to be covered by the insurer.

(e) "Prospectus" means a document issued by the insurer or in its behalf to the prospective buyers of insurance, and should contain such particulars as are mentioned in Rule 11 of Insurance Rules, 1939 and includes a brochure or leaflet serving the purpose. Such a document should also specify the type and character of riders on the main product indicating the nature of benefits flowing thereupon;

(f) Words and expressions used and not defined in these regulations, but defined in the Act, or the Life Insurance Corporation Act, 1956, (31 of 1956) or the General Insurance Business (Nationalisation) Act, 1972 (57 of 1972), or the Insurance Regulatory and Development Authority Act, 1999 (41 of 1999) or the Insurance Rules, 1939 shall have the meanings respectively assigned to them in those Acts or the Rules.

3. Point of Sale

(1) Notwithstanding anything mentioned in regulation 2(e) above, a prospectus of any insurance product shall clearly state the scope of benefits, the extent of insurance cover and in an explicit manner explain the warranties, exceptions and conditions of the insurance cover and, in case of life insurance, whether the product is participating (with-profits) or non-participating (without-profits). The allowable rider or riders on the product shall be clearly spelt out with regard to their scope of benefits, and in no case, the premium relatable to all the riders put together shall exceed 30% of the premium of the main product.
Explanation: The rider or riders attached to a life policy shall bear the nature and character of the main policy, viz. participating or non-participating and accordingly the life insurer shall make provisions, etc., in its books.

(2) An insurer or its agent or other intermediary shall provide all material information in respect of a proposed cover to the prospect to enable the prospect to decide on the best cover that would be in his or her interest.

(3) Where the prospect depends upon the advice of the insurer or his agent or an insurance intermediary, such a person must advise the prospect dispassionately.

(4) Where, for any reason, the proposal and other connected papers are not filled by the prospect, a certificate may be incorporated at the end of proposal form from the prospect that the contents of the form and documents have been fully explained to him and that he has fully understood the significance of the proposed contract.

(5) In the process of sale, the insurer or its agent or any intermediary shall act according to the code of conduct prescribed by:

  (i) the Authority,

  (ii) the Councils that have been established under section 64C of the Act, and

(iii) the recognized professional body or association of which the agent or intermediary or insurance intermediary is a member.

4. Proposal for Insurance

(1) Except in cases of a marine insurance cover, where current market practices do not insist on a written proposal form, in all cases, a proposal for grant of a cover, either for life business or for general business, must be evidenced by a written document. It is the duty of an insurer to furnish to the insured free of charge, within 30 days of the acceptance of a proposal, a copy of the proposal form.

(2) Forms and documents used in the grant of cover may, depending upon the circumstances of each case, be made available in languages recognised under the Constitution of India.

(3) In filling the form of proposal, the prospect is to be guided by the provisions of Section 45 of the Act. Any proposal form seeking information for grant of life cover may prominently state therein the requirements of Section 45 of the Act.

(4) Where a proposal form is not used, the insurer shall record the information obtained orally or in writing, and confirm it within a period of 15 days thereof with the proposer and incorporate the information in its cover note or policy. The onus of proof shall rest with the insurer in respect of any information not so recorded, where the insurer claims that the proposer suppressed any material information or provided misleading or false information on any matter material to the grant of a cover.

(5) Wherever the benefit of nomination is available to the proposer, in terms of the Act or the conditions of policy, the insurer shall draw the attention of the proposer to it and encourage the prospect to avail the facility.

(6) Proposals shall be processed by the insurer with speed and efficiency and all decisions thereof shall be

communicated by it in writing within a reasonable period not exceeding 15 days from receipt of proposals by the insurer.

5. Grievance Redressal Procedure

Every insurer shall have in place proper procedures and effective mechanism to address complaints and grievances of policyholders efficiently and with speed and the same along-with the information in respect of Insurance Ombudsman shall be communicated to the policyholder alongwith the policy document and as maybe found necessary.

6. Matters to be stated in Life Insurance Policy

(1) A life insurance policy shall clearly state:

- (a) the name of the plan governing the policy, its terms and conditions;
- (b) whether it is participating in profits or not;
- (c) the basis of participation in profits such as cash bonus, deferred bonus, simple or compound reversionary bonus;
- (d) the benefits payable and the contingencies upon which these are payable and the other terms and conditions of the insurance contract;
- (e) the details of the riders attaching to the main policy;
- (f) the date of commencement of risk and the date of maturity or date(s) on which the benefits are payable;
- (g) the premiums payable, periodicity of payment, grace period allowed for payment of the premium, the date the last instalment of premium, the implication of discontinuing the payment of an instalment(s) of premium and also the provisions of a guaranteed surrender value;
- (h) the age at entry and whether the same has been admitted;
- (i) the policy requirements for (a) conversion of the

policy into paid up policy, (b) surrender, (c) non-forfeiture, and (d) revival of lapsed policies;

(j) contingencies excluded from the scope of the cover, both in respect of the main policy and the riders;

(k) the provisions for nomination, assignment, and loans on security of the policy and a statement that the rate of interest payable on such loan amount shall be as prescribed by the insurer at the time of taking the loan;

(l) any special clauses or conditions, such as, first pregnancy clause, suicide clause etc.;

(m) the address of the insurer to which all communications in respect of the policy shall be sent; and

(n) the documents that are normally required to be submitted by a claimant in support of a claim under the policy.

(2) While acting under regulation 6(1) in forwarding the policy to the insured, the insurer shall inform by the letter forwarding the policy that he has a period of 15 days from the date of receipt of the policy document to review the terms and conditions of the policy and where the insured disagrees to any of those terms or conditions, he has the option to return the policy stating the reasons for his objection, when he shall be entitled to a refund of the premium paid, subject only to a deduction of a proportionate risk premium for the period on cover and the expenses incurred by the insurer on medical examination of the proposer and stamp duty charges.

(3) In respect of a unit linked policy, in addition to the deductions under sub-regulation (2) of this regulation, the insurer shall also be entitled to repurchase the unit at the price of the units on the date of cancellation.

(4) In respect of a cover, where premium charged is dependent on age, the insurer shall ensure that the age is admitted as far as possible before issuance of the policy document. In case where age has not been

admitted by the time the policy is issued, the insurer shall make efforts to obtain proof of age and admit the same as soon as possible.

7. Matters to be Stated in General Insurance Policy

(1) A general insurance policy shall clearly state:

(a) the name(s) and address(es) of the insured and of any bank(s) or any other person having financial interest in the subject matter of insurance;
(b) full description of the property or interest insured;
(c) the location or locations of the property or interest insured under the policy and, where appropriate, with respective insured values;
(d) period of Insurance;
(e) sums insured;
(f) perils covered and not covered;
(h) any franchise or deductible applicable;
(i) premium payable and where the premium is provisional subject to adjustment, the basis of adjustment of premium be stated;
(j) policy terms, conditions and warranties;
(k) action to be taken by the insured upon occurrence of a contingency likely to give rise to a claim under the policy;
(l) the obligations of the insured in relation to the subject matter of insurance upon occurrence of an event giving rise to a claim and the rights of the insurer in the circumstances;
(m) any special conditions attaching to the policy;
(n) provision for cancellation of the policy on grounds of mis-representation, fraud, non-disclosure of material facts or non-cooperation of the insured;
(o) the address of the insurer to which all communications in respect of the insurance contract should be sent;
(p) the details of the riders attaching to the main policy; and

(q) proforma of any communication the insurer may seek from the policyholders to service the policy.

(2) Every insurer shall inform and keep informed periodically the insured on the requirements to be fulfilled by the insured regarding lodging of a claim arising in terms of the policy and the procedures to be followed by him to enable the insurer to settle a claim early.

8. Claims procedure in respect of a life insurance policy

(1) A life insurance policy shall state the primary documents which are normally required to be submitted by a claimant in support of a claim.
(2) A life insurance company, upon receiving a claim, shall process the claim without delay. Any queries or requirement of additional documents, to the extent possible, shall be raised all at once and not in a piece-meal manner, within a period of 15 days of the receipt of the claim.
(3) A claim under a life policy shall be paid or be disputed giving all the relevant reasons, within 30 days from the date of receipt of all relevant papers and clarifications required. However, where the circumstances of a claim warrant an investigation in the opinion of the insurance company, it shall initiate and complete such investigation at the earliest. Where in the opinion of the insurance company the circumstances of a claim warrant an investigation, it shall initiate and complete such investigation at the earliest, in any case not later than 6 months from the time of lodging the claim.
(4) Subject to the provisions of section 47 of the Act, where a claim is ready for payment but the payment cannot be made due to any reasons of a proper identification of the payee, the life insurer shall hold the amount for the benefit of the payee and such an amount shall earn interest at the rate applicable to a savings bank account with a scheduled bank (effective from 30 days

following the submission of all papers and information).

(5) Where there is a delay on the part of the insurer in processing a claim for a reason other than the one covered by sub-regulation (4), the life insurance company shall pay interest on the claim amount at a rate which is 2% above the bank rate prevalent at the beginning of the financial year in which the claim is reviewed by it.

9. Claim Procedure in Respect of a General Insurance Policy

(1) An insured or the claimant shall give notice to the insurer of any loss arising under contract of insurance at the earliest or within such extended time as may be allowed by the insurer. On receipt of such a communication, a general insurer shall respond immediately and give clear indication to the insured on the procedures that he should follow. In cases where a surveyor has to be appointed for assessing a loss/ claim, it shall be so done within 72 hours of the receipt of intimation from the insured.

(2) Where the insured is unable to furnish all the particulars required by the surveyor or where the surveyor does not receive the full cooperation of the insured, the insurer or the surveyor as the case may be, shall inform in writing the insured about the delay that may result in the assessment of the claim. The surveyor shall be subjected to the code of conduct laid down by the Authority while assessing the loss, and shall communicate his findings to the insurer within 30 days of his appointment with a copy of the report being furnished to the insured, if he so desires. Where, in special circumstances of the case, either due to its special and complicated nature, the surveyor shall under intimation to the insured, seek an extension from the insurer for submission of his report. In no case shall a surveyor take more than six months from the date of his appointment to furnish his report.

(3) If an insurer, on the receipt of a survey report, finds that it is incomplete in any respect, he shall require the surveyor under intimation to the insured, to furnish an additional report on certain specific issues as may be required by the insurer. Such a request may be made by the insurer within 15 days of the receipt of the original survey report.
Provided that the facility of calling for an additional report by the insurer shall not be resorted to more than once in the case of a claim.

(4) The surveyor on receipt of this communication shall furnish an additional report within three weeks of the date of receipt of communication from the insurer.

(5) On receipt of the survey report or the additional survey report, as the case may be, an insurer shall within a period of 30 days offer a settlement of the claim to the insured. If the insurer, for any reasons to be recorded in writing and communicated to the insured, decides to reject a claim under the policy, it shall do so within a period of 30 days from the receipt of the survey report or the additional survey report, as the case may be.

(6) Upon acceptance of an offer of settlement as stated in sub-regulation (5) by the insured, the payment of the amount due shall be made within 7 days from the date of acceptance of the offer by the insured. In the cases of delay in the payment, the insurer shall be liable to pay interest at a rate which is 2% above the bank rate prevalent at the beginning of the financial year in which the claim is reviewed by it.

10. Policyholders' Servicing

(1) An insurer carrying on life or general business, as the case may be, shall at all times, respond within 10 days of the receipt of any communication from its policyholders in all matters, such as:

(a) recording change of address;

(b) noting a new nomination or change of nomination under a policy;
(c) noting an assignment on the policy;
(d) providing information on the current status of a policy indicating matters, such as, accrued bonus, surrender value and entitlement to a loan;
(e) processing papers and disbursal of a loan on security of policy;
(f) issuance of duplicate policy;
(g) issuance of an endorsement under the policy; noting a change of interest or sum assured or perils insured, financial interest of a bank and other interests; and
(h) guidance on the procedure for registering a claim and early settlement thereof.

11. General

(1) The requirements of disclosure of "material information" regarding a proposal or policy apply, under these regulations, both to the insurer and the insured.
(2) The policyholder shall assist the insurer, if the latter so requires, in the prosecution of a proceeding or in the matter of recovery of claims which the insurer has against third parties.
(3) The policyholder shall furnish all information that is sought from him by the insurer and also any other information which the insurer considers as having a bearing on the risk to enable the latter to assess properly the risk sought to be covered by a policy.
(4) Any breaches of the obligations cast on an insurer or insurance agent or insurance intermediary in terms of these regulations may enable the Authority to initiate action against each or all of them, jointly or severally, under the Act and/or the Insurance Regulatory and Development Authority Act, 1999.

ANNEXURE 8

DESCRIPTION OF DIFFERENT TYPES OF INSURANCE PLANS (PRODUCTS)

Term Insurance

Term insurance provides risk coverage on the insured's life. There is no cash reserve or investment portion in this type of policy and hence can be called pure insurance that simply provides coverage on the insured's life and pays the coverage amount on death during the period of coverage. No returns or monetary benefits are available if the insured survives the term of the policy or cancels the policy mid-term. A product can be purchased that increases annually, or the premium can be locked in for five, 10, 15, 20, or even 30 years. The premiums are lower than those for other products and this plan is most appropriate for needs that will decline or be eliminated over time. A variation of this policy is renewable and convertible and locks in the insured's future insurability. In other words, the insured may convert the term to another product in the future, regardless of health.

Whole Life Insurance

This is the most traditional life insurance product on the market. For a stipulated premium, the insurance company guarantees the insured's death benefit and cash values in the contract. The cash value of an insurance contract is the cash amount offered to the policy owner upon cancellation of the contract. Cash values are usually agreed for the case of premature cancellations in those forms of insurance contracts in which a portion of the premiums go toward an investment, like whole life insurance or endowment life insurance and other forms of permanent life insurance. Such amounts are often certain to be paid, either in case of death or in case of survival, and therefore not under risk. The contract determines for each possible cancellation date the related cash value. If the investment of premiums is contractually made in an individual account, the cash value is the value of the investments in that account at any particular time. Such cash value credited to an individual account during the tenure of the policy keeps growing with every payment of premium. The cost of insurance or mortality charges are frozen at issue, and the investment risk of the cash values is assumed by the company. Although the premium cost is usually higher than other permanent products, other benefits are provided. The death benefit will increase as cash values increase, premiums may disappear in the future based upon dividend performance, and loans may be used to borrow premiums in the future to keep the policy going should circumstances change.

Endowment

Endowments are policies in which the cash value built up inside the policy, equals the death benefit (face amount) at a certain age. The age this commences is known as the endowment age. Endowments are considerably more expensive (in terms of annual premiums) than either whole life or term. Endowment Insurance is paid out whether the insured lives through or dies within a specific period (e.g. 15 years) or a specific age (e.g. 65).

Unit Linked Insurance Plans

ULIP is term insurance tacked on to a mutual fund. It has flexible death benefits and premiums. The premiums are split into two distinct parts. One portion that goes for risk coverage that provides a term plan like death benefit and another portion that goes towards investments that build the cash value. The investment is denoted as units and is represented by the value that it has attained called as Net Asset Value (NAV). The cash values are a function of the underlying investment portfolios selected by the policyholder. The insurance companies offer as many as five to 10 different mutual fund companies along with their corresponding fund choices as underlying investment portfolios that can be chosen. The policy-owner therefore retains investment risk and control with respect to this portion of the plan.

ANNEXURE 9

CORRESPONDING PREMIUM INCREASE TO DIFFERENT EMRS FOR DIFFERENT AGES AND PLANS

Age	Plan	Class 2 EMR + 25	3+50	4+75	5+100	6+125
(1)	(2)	(3)	(4)	(5)	(6)	(7)
21-30	Term	25	50	75	100	125
	WLP	6.25%-8.75%	12.5%-17.5%	18.75%-26.25%	25%-35%	31.25%-43.75%
	Endow	2.5%-3.75%	5%-7. 5%	7.5%-11.25%	10%-15%	12.5%-18.75%
31-35	Term	25	50	75	100	125
	WLP	7.5%-10%	15%-20%	22.5%-30%	30%-40%	37.5%-50%
	Endow	7.5%-11.25%	10%-15%	12.5%-18.75%	2.5%-3.75%	5%-7. 5%
36-40	Term	25	50	75	100	125
	WLP	7.5%-11.25%	15%-22.5%	22.5%-33.75%	30%-45%	37.5%-56.25%
	Endow	7.5%-15%	10%-20%	12.5%-25%	2.5%-5%	5%-10%
41-45	Term	25	50	75	100	125
	WLP	8.75%-12.5%	17.5%-25%	26.25%-37.5%	35%-50%	43.75%-62.5%
	Endow	3.75%-6.25%	11.25%-18.75%	15%-25%	18.75%-31.25%	7.5%-12.5%

(Contd.)

ANNEXURE 1 (*Contd.*)

(1)	*(2)*	*(3)*	*(4)*	*(5)*	*(6)*	*(7)*
46-50	Term	25	50	75	100	125
	WLP	8.75%-15%	17.5%-30%	26.25%-45%	35%-60%	43.75%-75%
	Endow	3.75%-6.25%	11.25%-18.75%	15%-25 %	18.75%-31.25%	7.5% 12.5 %
51-55	Term	25	50	75	100	125
	WLP	8.75%-16.25%	17.5%-32.5%	26.25%-48.75%	35%-65%	43.75%-81.25%
	Endow	5%-6.25%	15%-18.75%	20%-25%	25%-31.25%	10%-12.5%
56-60	Term	25	50	75	100	125
	WLP	10%-17.5%	20%-35%	30%-52.5%	40%-70%	50%-87.5%
	Endow	5%-6.25%	15%-18.75%	20%-25%	25%-31.25%	10%-12. 5%

You can notice that for term plan all percentages increases are the same as EMR. This is because the entire premium is being taken as mortality premium and increased as per the EMR.

Example

Mr. Madhur is 25 years of age. He has diabetes and based on his history, test reports and doctors assessment the underwriter decides that the risk of death due to various complications of diabetes are more than that of an average healthy person. The underwriter further evaluates the case and concludes that the extra mortality is 100% based on various parameters. The premium increase for different plans will be as follows:

Term plan = Premium Rs. 1000
Rated (Loaded) Premium = 100% × 1000 = Rs. 2000

Endowment Plan = Premium Rs. 4000
Rated (Loaded) Premium = 10 to 15% × 4000 = Rs. 4400 to 4600
(As per table of endowment above for ages between 21 to 30 years for 100% EMR the range of premium increase is between 10 to 15%)

Whole life Plan = Premium Rs. 3000
Rated (Loaded) Premium = 25% to 35% × 3000 = Rs. 3750 to 4050

As per table of whole life above for ages between 21 to 30 years for 100% EMR the range of premium increase is between 25 to 35%)

In the above example it is seen that in case of term plan the premium has doubled but for other plans the increase has been less.

For the same person if the underwriter decides that the extra mortality is + 50 EMR that is 1.5 times of the premium then the premium for different plans will be as follows:

Term plan = Premium Rs. 1000
Loaded Premium = 1.5 × 1000 = Rs. 1500
Endowment Plan = Premium 4000
Loaded Premium = 1.05 to 1.075 (5-7.5%) × 4000 = Rs. 4200 to 4300
Whole Life Plan = Premium 3000
Loaded Premium = 1.125 – 1.175 (12.5% – 17.5%) × 3000 = Rs. 3375 to 3525

Bibliography

Actuarial Standards Board, Actuarial Standard of Practice, No. 12, Risk Classification (for All Practice Areas), Revised Edition, Developed by the Task Force to Revise ASOP No. 12 of the General Committee of the Actuarial Standards Board Adopted by the ctuarial Standards Board, December 2005, Doc. No. 101.

AIDS and the Moral Economy of Insurance by Deborah Stone, The American Prospect Online Edition.

An Insurer's Duty to Investigate by John Dwight Ingram Florida State University, College of Law.

Bridging the Gap Between Life Insurer and Consumer in the Genetic Testing Era: The RF Proposal, *Indiana Law Journal,* 74(4) Fall 1999 by Christopher M. Keefer.

CFP2, Risk Management and Insurance Planning, International College of Financial Planning Limited, 2002.

Insurance Underwriting: A Managerial Perspective, Vol. I, 2002, ICFAI University Press.

Insurance Underwriting: A Managerial Perspective, Vol. III, 2002, ICFAI University Press.

Insurance Underwriting: A Managerial Perspective, Vol. III, 2002, ICFAI University Press.

International Underwriting Challenges and Opportunities, Brad Gabel, CLU, FALU, FLMI, Vice President and Chief Underwriter, AIG Life Brokerage, http://www.nailba.com/educationalprograms/monthlyeducation/200604education.pdf

Introduction to Risk Management and Insurance, Eighth Edition by Mark S. Dorfman, 2005, Prentice-Hall Inc.

Life Underwriting Newsletter, Second issue of the Munich Re- Life Underwriting Newsletter.

McGill's Life Insurance, Fifth Edition, Edward E. Graves, Editor, Lynn Hayes, Managing Editor, The American College Press, 2004.

Occupation Underwriting—A new Perspective, John Turner General Cologne Re, Risk Insights, November 2000, Vol. 4, No. 5.

Overview of Financial Underwriting by Wayne Macedo, Vice-President and Chief Underwriter, International Division, Transamerica Reinsurance.

Peter Maynard, Taking the Art out of Underwriting viewed on website http://www.allfinanz.com/

Selection of Risks, American Viewpoint and Practice, by Andrew C. Webster, F.F.A., F.S.A., A.I.A. (Submitted to the Faculty on 19th January 1959).

Social Trends #64: January 5, 2004, Suicide in Japan: Part Two—The Impact of the Suicide Rate on Life Insurance Policies, J. Sean Curtin (Fellow, GLOCOM) and Earl H. Kinmonth (Professor, Taisho University).

Swiss Re/Cologne Re rating manual.

T.S. Ramakrishna Rao, *IRDA Journal*, Oct. 2006.

The Impact of Tele-Underwriting on Mortality Experience, By Jonathan Crumiller, Chief Operating Officer and Tele-Underwriting Practice Leader, Spring 2006, Princeton Consultants, Tele Underwriting Practice.

Underwriting Guide for Financial Advisers including an Occupation and Sports and Pastimes Guide for Disability Benefits, Freinds Provident.

Underwriting Quick reference Guide, Legal and General Assurance Society Limited.

Index